AZOO

The Story and History
of the Pilot Gigs of Cornwall
and the Isles of Scilly 1666–1993

AZOOK!

In Richard Gillis' *The Pilot gigs of Cornwall and the Isles of Scilly* Gillis recounts the tradition of Newquay gig crews being started with the old cry what went up when the shoals of pilchards were sighted. He gives that word as "Hubba" but the word was actually "Hevva"! as in "Hevva Cake" the traditional currant laden sugar dusted cake often sold as "heavy" cake in Cornish bakeries. "Hevva!" was also the title of a book I wrote in 1983, so it was appropriate when I read that if further energy was required the cry became 'AZOOK.'

Gillis says that whilst he could not discover the origins of this word he felt it was an appropriate echo from the past working days of the old pilot gigs. I felt that it would also make an appropriate title for my book.

AZOOK!

*The Story and History
of the Pilot Gigs of Cornwall
and the Isles of Scilly 1666–1993*

Keith Harris

DYLLANSOW TRURAN

Published by Dyllansow Truran.
Trewolsta, Trewirgie, Redruth, Cornwall.

ISBN 185022075 1

Typeset by Kestrel Data, Exeter
Printed in Great Britain by Short Run Press Ltd, Exeter

Contents

Acknowledgements

I would like to thank the following people for their help, advice, photographs, and other materials used in the compilation of this book.

Len Truran, Frank Gibson, Mr Knight and his excellent staff at the Local Studies Department at Redruth Library. Roger Penhallurick at the Royal Institute of Cornwall, Truro. Christopher Barrett, Paul Harris and Michael Williams of the Hayle Pilot Gig Club, Jack Buzza of Truro, all of whom have made photographs available to me.

I would also like to thank Barbara James for typing the bulk of my manuscript and Diane Lowman for typing some sections.

Most of all I would like to thank my wife Valerie for her tolerance and patience whilst I have been absorbed in researching and writing.

Keith Harris
CARN ARTHEN 1994

Beaching a gig

Introduction

The Peters family of St. Mawes, Tiddy and Gluyas of Scilly, Burt of St. Michaels Mount, Simmons of Penzance, the Tredwens of Padstow and many other unknown or unrecorded shipwrights, built many hundreds of gigs mainly during the 18th and 19th centuries.

These gigs carried out many many thousands of pilotage duties successfully and without incident and were probably raced for fun as well as for employment. However, it is for the comparatively few, spectacular wreck and rescue and particularly salvage, that were part of everyday life both on mainland Cornwall and the Isles of Scilly that the gigs are recorded and remembered by. Tales of wreckers luring ships ashore are a hopeless and scandalous lie. Cornishmen and Scillonians had no need to lure ships ashore they came ashore with such amazing regularity on all parts of the coast there was no need for anyone to lure them!

A prayer attributed to John Troutbeck a St. Marys parson from 1780–1795 ran:-

"We pray thee Lord, *NOT* that wrecks should happen *BUT*, that if any wrecks should happen, Thou will guide them into the Scilly Isles, for the benefit of the inhabitants". The Revd. Troutbeck, himself was forced to resign for handling contraband.

Wrecking was seen as a legitimate bounty from the sea and the gig was perhaps the finest all round vessel ever designed for both speed, seaworthiness and capacity for carrying, combined with a shallow draught, and with a crew of 6 plus a cox, considerable power.

On the mainland A. G. Folliott, author of a book called "The Cornish Coasts and Moors", once asked an old pilot what he thought could be done to prevent the many wrecks that occurred around the Lizard and Manacles area, he replied "If only they would sink Lloyds signalling station, there would be no more wrecks on the Manacles or around Lizard Head because Captains would give that corner a wide berth". These appear to have been prophetic words for since the Lloyds signalling station closed in 1969 there have been no major shipping losses on either the Lizard or the Manacles.

The pilot gigs of Cornwall and the Isles of Scilly were probably never designed but were the result of perhaps centuries of evolution, each gig being a refinement of its predecessors. However it is generally agreed that this process reached its zenith in 1838 when William Peters created the gig *Treffry* for owners in Newquay of the same name. This gig has not only never been improved on, she is to this day being copied; almost all the new gigs built in recent years have been clones of the *Treffry*, which is still afloat and is rowed regularly by the Newquay Rowing Club.

Gig racing which started with crews racing for pilotage work is now a feature of Cornish Life; almost every coastal town and village either has a gig or has plans to acquire one. Several have been built in the USA, and who knows perhaps one year soon the annual World Pilot Gig Championship will become a truly International affair.

I hope that the young people of today and tomorrow who row the gigs for sport, fun and leisure are aware of the ancestry of these fine craft and of the blood, sweat and tears that have been shed both by our fore fathers who worked in them and by the families that have been left at home to grieve when the gigs did not return to their safe havens or did so without a full crew.

THE PETER'S OF
ST. MAWES

William Peters of St. Mawes, founder of the gig building dynasty

Almost every gig in existence has a bit of the legacy of William Peters in its pedigree. Either it was built by a member of the Peters family or by someone trained by a Peters or, in the case of all the gigs built in the twentieth century, which have all been built from plans and moulds taken from a Peters gig.

The longevity of the old pilot gigs is phenomenal when one considers their lightweight construction and the hard usage they had in their working lives, and continue to have as leisure/racing craft. The planking in the gigs seldom excedes ¼". Yet many gigs from the William and Nicholas Peters era survive from (as in the case of the *Newquay*) as far back as 1812. Which was three years before the battle of Waterloo and only seven years after Nelson's famous sea battle at Trafalgar. In fact the *Newquay* was built in the same year as Nelson's flagship *Victory* was withdrawn from the active list of the Royal Navy. Unlike H.M.S. *Victory*, *Newquay* has not become a museum exhibit, although she has had the odd repair, she is still largely original and is still rowed regularly by members of the Newquay Rowing Club who own and maintain her. Other gigs built by the Peters family that also survive include:

Dove built by William Peters 1820 also at Newquay
Bonnet built by William Peters 1830 kept in Scilly
Slippen built by William Peters 1830 kept in Scilly
Treffry built by William Peters 1838 kept at Newquay
Golden Eagle built by Nicholas Peters 1870 kept in Scilly
Shah built by Nicholas Peters 1873 kept in Scilly
Sussex Peters built in 1886 Rebuilt and owned by Ralph Bird 1971
Campernell Peters built in 1895 Renovated at Falmouth College 1993

All these gigs are still in commission and must comprise one of the most unique collections of veterans attributable to one family and one yard anywhere in the world.

That they remain for us to admire and use today rather than having gone the way of so many others is due largely to the zeal, conviction, hard work and perseverance of a small group of enthusiasts from the Newquay Rowing Club who, in the 1950's set about rescuing and restoring what gigs could be saved in the Isles of Scilly. Foremost amongst these was R. H. C. Gillis a Newquay Pharmacist. R. H. C. Gillis' love of the Cornish pilot gigs started in his childhood and lasted the whole of his life. At the age of 14 he was rowing bow oar in the Newquay gig *Dove*. In 1828 he was a member of the crew which included:- W. J. Kennedy stroke oar, W. J. Jenkin bow oar, E. Hoare at No. 2, J. Reynolds No. 3, W. Trebilcock No. 4 and R. H. C. Gillis No. 5 with W. R. Coumbe as coxswain when they rowed against crews from Fowey and Polruan over a timed and measure mile in a record breaking time of 6 minutes and 15 seconds. (Also in the Peters built gig *Dove*)

In the 1950's, (as I have mentioned), R. H. C. Gillis, in the company of George Northey and Tom Pryor visited the Scillies and purchased several old gigs, *Shah*, *Golden Eagle*, *Bonnet* and *Slippen*, had them shipped back to the mainland and eventually arranged for them to be renovated, all of these gigs have since been returned to Scilly where they formed the nucleus of the revival of interest in gig racing, not only in Scilly but also on the mainland.

Other gigs rescued by other clubs did not fare so well, *Zelda* and *Gipsy* both of which went to Padstow, were, after a brief revival, destroyed. *Zelda* was crushed beyond repair when a lorry backed into her on the quay of Padstow in the 1950's and *Gipsy*, (which incidentally was the last gig to be used to put a pilot, Jack Hicks of St. Agnes aboard a ship, the *Foremost* on 22nd December, 1939), was burned on 27th May, 1964.

Richard Gillis was at hand to observe this sad spectacle and did, in fact, salvage a rudder pintle from the *Gipsy*, which was later used on *Newquay*.

Gillis' love and knowledge of the gigs was also expressed in many articles, booklets and features in local magazines. His work has been widely used by others who have used his knowledge and experience in works of their own, indeed I doubt if this effort of mine would have been possible had Richard Gillis not committed his knowledge of the gigs to print.

Now to get back to the Peters family. The Peters established their yard at Polvarth, near St. Mawes around 1790. The cottage bearing this date was converted from an old salt store by the Peters family in 1790. At the same time as the Peters were converting the salt store, they received their first order for a six oared pilot gig. There is some speculation where the gig was destined for, but it was probably ordered for Padstow where it was to be used as a lifeboat, legend has it that it was commissioned by a member of the clergy. There are records of a six oared gig being kept at Padstow, as a lifeboat in a shed or house thirty feet long.

The Peters yard is still in existence, though no longer owned by a Peters, the last member of that family, Frank, sold the yard a few years ago; it is now called the Freshwater boat yard.

William Peters, the founder, built all kinds of craft at the yard, schooners, pilot cutters, fishing boats, four and six oared gigs, ships, boats and punts.

One schooner built at the yard was well known locally, called the *Olive Branch* she was a very beautiful example of the shipwrights art. However, because of the relatively high price that could be demanded for gig building, the yard eventually specialised in this type of craft; often building two at a time, except when an order for a specially designed gig was received.

All the gigs of the fast, high class type, rather than the run of the mill kind, were launched with a great deal of ceremony, the crew that manned them at the launch wore red jackets and stove-pipe hats (garments that could still be found in the Peter's sheds in the 1960's. When *Treffry* was launched in 1838 she was ceremonially rowed around the Carrick Roads and a warship at anchor dipped her ensign in salute to the gaily clad crew of the gig. Gigs built by Nicholas Peters were priced at a £1 per foot in 1870; that was the price of the *Golden Eagle*, the oars, masts, spars and sails were all extra. This was an incredible price, William Paynter a St. Ives boatbuilder and contemporary of both William Peters and Nicholas Peters was charging the following prices:

1864 *Margarets* punt 15' 6'' long £7
1864 Captain Anthony's boat *Palace* 15' 6'' £9
1864 Punt 12 ft long to the Kate Roach £6.50
1865 New 17 ft boat to *Queen of the Sea* £12

In 1900 the hull of a 40 foot lugger could be obtained for about £80 this would be for a vessel of about 12-15 tons approx. 12 foot beam and drawing about 6' 6''. Gigs were always built very lightly to give them as much speed advantage as possible. A typical 32'0'' x 4' 9'' gig will only weigh about 7 hundred weight and could, if needs dictated, be carried by her crew.

Whilst most of the boats built by the Peters were for a local market either on the Cornish mainland or for the Isles of Scilly; they also went further afield. The Peters built gigs for both Lloyds the insurance company and also for the Coastguard and Preventive service. In 1812 the Peters built gig *Newquay* was one of three gigs built for shipment to Bassein, an inland port on the Irrawaddy Delta in Burma. Of the three ordered only two were sent, no transport could be found for the third gig. She was subsequently purchased by W. Broad and Sons of Falmouth who were in their first years as Lloyds agents, having opened for business in November 1811. They in turn sold the gig to pilots in Newquay who Christened the gig after their home port. The two gigs transported to Bassein were, apparently still in use in 1937. It would be fascinating to see if they are still in existence.

Occasionally the poachers became game keepers, some gigs were used by the Preventive Service to apprehend would be smugglers. Records show that many Preventive service stations were equipped with either a four or six oared gig or a galley. Portscatho for example had both a four and a six oared gig both equipped with oars and a lugsail main and mizzen. Both these gigs were built by Peters of St. Mawes. In March 1827 the Portscatho station ordered a new four oared gig from William Peters and in the same month he is on record as having repaired the Gerrans boats.

The Peter's family selected and felled their own timber for their boats. Presumably much of it coming from the Roseland Peninsula or from the many woodlands on the Fal. The timber used was the narrow or small leaf Cornish elm, and trunks selected had to be of a size to produce planking for gigs of around 30 ft. The Peters would only use one scarf or join in each plank and would only use mature trees. There was a belief that old trees produced old worn out wood.

The timber baulks were either hauled, or more likely floated, to Polvarth where they were submerged in the creek mud, held down by heavy chains. The elm butts remained in the creek mud for 5 years before being removed and pit sawn by a sawyer who used to come over from Penryn in a hand worked paddle boat. The elm butts were sawn into planks which must have been only slightly thicker than their finished ¼" or so. This work was highly skilled, to maintain a consistently accurate cut was no mean feat. According to R. H. C. Gillis the saw would progress through a trunk at a rate of up to a foot per stroke. Legend has it that the Peters sawpits were also used as cock fighting pits on Sundays and holidays.

It is interesting to note that in 1953, when Newquays gig *Dove* was refitted, that Frank Peters made the discovery that she had been built of broad leaf elm which is less flexible and heavier than narrow leaf elm. Edgar March speculates that this may account for her being a "dirty" boat in heavy weather.

Once cut, the boards were then stacked to air dry for another 12 months before being used. The keels and timbers were of American (Rock) Elm, which was chosen to produce a faster stronger boat on account of its lightness and greater flexibility. When Slippen, built about 1830 was repaired in 1953, a length of bilge planking, some say 4', Gillis says 6' long, was removed, it could be bent to form a complete circle and when released would spring back to shape without the slightest distortion, or damage. However elm was not always the wood used. In the case of *Newquay*; when her keel was renewed in 1955, it was found that her keel was in fact of oak.

In 1955 a ground sea filled *Treffry* in Newquay harbour and consequently caused her to leak to such a degree that it was decided that only a new keel would sort her out. The search for a suitable 32' length of either oak, narrow leaf elm or American Rock Elm went from one end of the country to the other without success. Finally Mr. Henry Moreland of the Gloucester timber and match company took up the quest finally locating a baulk of oak from the Clanna Estate in Gloucestershire. Henry Moreland generously donated the 9 cwt. baulk of oak, with its delivery free of charge. The timber ultimately provided new keels for *Treffry*, *Dove*, *Slippen*, *Golden Eagle*, and *Bonnet* as well as a keel for the Padstow gig *Zelda*, and new gunwales for Bonnet and *Golden Eagle*.

Iron bolts forged locally (by Sam Hooker in the Peters time) were always used in gigs built by the Peters family for fastening deadwoods, because in such long slender boats there was a danger of copper fastenings stretching when the boats were being handled on shore, or when flexing in a sea way.

Copper roves for the rivets were hand made, cut from a sheet of copper with tin shears and the holes punched in to take the nails. When fitted the roves were always set with the corners North, South, East, West, rather than with the top and bottom edges parallel to the keel, in order to shed, rather than hold any water, which may cause corrosion. It is a fact, that apart from the odd replaced timber, the *Newquay*, *Treffry* and *Dove* have never been renailed, whereas *Golden Eagle* has been renailed twice, once in 1910 and again when brought to Newquay in 1953. Shah was also found to be nailsick. Interestingly nails taken from *Newquay* built 1812, together with nails from *Shah* built 1873 and *Golden Eagle* built 1870 were sent to Camborne School of Mines for analysis. The copper nails from *Newquay* and *Treffry's*

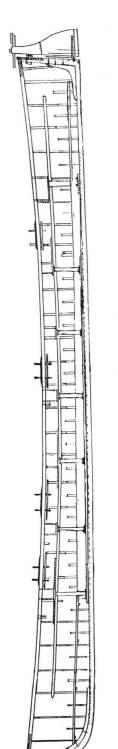

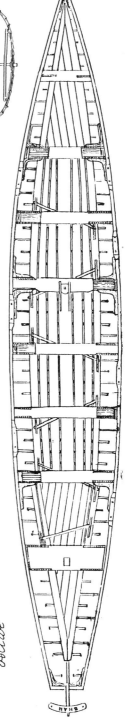

The St.Agnes gig "Shah", built in 1873 by Nicholas Peters of
St.Mawes. She was originally built for the Pilots of
St.Ives who refused her because they considered her to be
too fine in the bow. Shah measures 30'2¼" x 4'9" and despite
losing her first race to put a pilot aboard a ship, she has
always been considered to be a fast gig. Newquay Rowing Club
bought her in 1953 and had much work done on her in 1955. In 1963
"Shah" returned, on loan to Scilly and in 1974 was exchanged for a new gig
"Active"

copper fastenings could have all have come from Cornish sources. Angarrack, near Hayle, had a copper smelting operation which was in business from 1704–1881. round rooves or roves did not come into manufacture until 1850–60. However, it could also be that it was the practice when the gigs were in pilot service, to paint the gigs black, and in order to improve performance they were often black-leaded below the water line. One of the practices of the time, to produce a sheen on the black lead, was to mix it and polish with vinegar; and it is very probable that it was the impregnation of the boards with vinegar, that had, over the years, caused the nails to be eaten away. When Golden Eagle was worked on in 1953 her fastenings were found to have wasted away to the size of pins.

In 1955 Steve Brabyn and his assistant shipwright Donald McBirnie fitted new keels to Newquay and Shah. The timber a length of small leaf elm was found at Grampound Road. When the keels of *Shah* and *Newquay* were fitted there was much speculation as to whether this could be done without removing either one or both garboards. Mr. Brabyn did achieve this difficult task on *Shah* without removing either garboard and his assistant Donald McBirnie was able to repeat the operation on *Newquay*, albeit with frequent instructional bulletins from Mr. Brabyn, who had been taken ill, and sent directions from his sick bed.

When building gigs, nails were ragged or barbed with a chisel before being driven into a pre-drilled hole. The hole was usually drilled with a spade-ended drill made from a piece of unbrella steel, using an old fashioned whimbrel, which looks like the handle of an old fashioned spinning top, with a chuck at the end instead of a top.

Gillis and Edgar March maintain that the notched or joggled timbers shaped to fit the overlapping clinker planks were prepared before the timbers were steamed and fitted, however, shipwrights such as John Gardner and Howard Chapelle, both say the technique for joggled frames is to fit them hot and temporarily secure them. When set and cold the inside laps are scribed on the frames. They are then removed shaped, then refitted and fastened. Chapelle says "that the extra work of making these frames is warranted only when the boat is used for landing on rough beaches. The extra support given to the planking, between laps, by joggled frames is desirable under such conditions. Joggled frames are often used in large lap strake hulls".

Garboard planks were fitted to the keel in a ⅜" rabbet, then skewnailed into the keel. No hogpiece was used so as to maintain a high degree of watertight integrity and great flexibility. Many fishermen working from the small coves demanded similar construction.

However, when repairs were undertaken on the old gigs in the

The gig Shah rescued by R.H.C. Gillis. George Northey and Tom Pryor before, (top picture) and after, (bottom picture) its renovation at Brabyn's yard Padstow

1950's, Hogs were fitted to two of the old boats. Shah had a hog of American Elm fitted in three pieces scarphed together, one piece being slid in the gap created by the garboard plank being removed for a 12 foot long section to replace the damage done by a sharp stone some 40 years previously. When the hog piece was completed and the garboard was repaired, they were both doubled with pine to ensure she was absolutely watertight.

When Newquays new keel was fitted in 1955 by Donald McBirnie, it was decided to fit a hog to help cure her leaking. The hog was fitted in two pieces and was slightly chamfered where it met the garboards to form a caulking seal. When Shah was repaired she required, in addition to having almost a wheelbarrow full of paint being burnt off, 54 new timbers, 8 new thwarts with knees and the new keel and hog as previously mentioned.

Bonnet when she was built by Peters in 1830 for St. Martins pilots, had a beam of 5' 0½''. She was then sold to Tresco and later to Ernie and Sampson Jenkins on Bryher, where she hung for years strung up to the tie beams in *Golden Eagle's* gig house. The heat, and lack of use caused her planks to shrink and crack. Later still she was sold again to Tresco and Obediah Hicks took out her thwarts and "pulled her home" changing her beam from 5'0½'' to 4' 9¾''. Apart from having 32 new timbers and a false keel fitted in 1953 when she was brought from Scilly to Newquay, she was subsequently sent to Brabyns at Padstow in 1956 to have a strake removed, have new risings put in and the thwarts were lowered, at the same time a new keel, cut from the length of oak supplied by Mr. Moreland was also fitted.

When *Slippen* was purchased by Newquay in 1953 her planking was sound but many of her timbers had been broken in her 123 year life. Altogether 23 long and 16 short timbers were replaced as well as other minor repairs.

Gillis and March both mention the Peters shipwrights practice of coating all surfaces of joints with whale oil from a bottle with a feather. Mr. Gillis recalls in 1954 seeing the remains of a Peters built gig called *Gleaner* which had recently been dismantled by Obediah Hicks and his son Ivor. *Gleaner* would have been over a hundred years old at this time and Gillis reports that the joints he inspected were just like new.

William and Nicholas Peters had a very strict practice regarding the colours of their gigs. Like the Ford Motor Companies paint policy with their Model T. Fords, i.e. "you can have any colour as long it's black". The Peters policy was no matter what colour was ordered, all their gigs were painted white! The only other finish available was varnish. When *Treffry* was built, her builders thought her to be their

11

The Newquay crew, who, in 1928, rowing the gig Dove against crews from Polruan and Fowey on a measured mile course off Trevelgue Head, set a record time of 6 minutes 15 seconds. The crew consisting of W. E. Kennedy, W. J. Jenkins, E. Hoare, J. Reynolds, W. Trebilcock, R. H. C. Gillis and W. R. Coumbe. R. H. C. Gillis is pictured 3 in from the left. This crew also won the Howitt Trophy in 1938

R. H. C. Gillis pictured rowing bow oar, W. J. Jenkin rowing stroke oar and J. C. Carrivick pair of paddles this crew were Randan Champions in 1924, 1925 and 1926

finest creation to date and were so proud of her that instead of painting her, she was polished with linseed oil. On being launched, *Treffry* was rowed past a warship in Falmouth harbour and the captain had the Man'O'War's ensign dipped in salute.

Thwarts in Peter's build gigs were all quite thin at approx. ¾" and needed support from a central post which had the effect of creating a light upward curve in the thwarts. This was to serve two purposes, first to help create a tension in the gig and add to its flexibility and strength and secondly to prevent a thwart being pushed through the gigs ¼" planking if she came alongside a ship too forcefully. The bow in the thwart would, in such an event, bend to a greater degree. To prevent thwart knees from breaking under such strains, downward nails were only clinched rather than rivetted like the side nails.

In their working days, gigs used oars or sweeps of ash some of them up to 18' 0" in length. These were used, in the words of the old saying with a "long and strong" sweeping stroke and it seems that this technique, whilst fine for long distance rowing has been super-ceded by the use of shorter oars 13' to 14' 6" and a quicker stroke. Spooned blades were also found to be more effective than the old flat bladed sweeps. Modern *paddles* are made, if possible, of silver spruce or of laminated timber to combine strength with lightness. The thin gunwales and light construction of a gig precludes the use of rowlocks. If they were used and a rower "caught a crab" (or missed his stroke) he would probably smash the gunwale. To avoid this thole pins are used, they are usually used in a combination of one hardwood and one pinewood pin per oar. In 1953 a silver spruce paddle cost £3.50. In 1993 a similar paddle would cost in excess of £100!!

It is reckoned that an ordinary crew could row a gig at about 8 miles per hour on flat water. *Czar* has been recorded as having covered the 1½ miles from Carn, near to St. Mary's Pier in 11 minutes or 7 minutes and 20 seconds for the mile.

Dolphin has covered a mile in an estimated 7 minutes and 18 seconds.

In 1928 a Newquay crew comprising of W. E. Kennedy, W. J. Jenkin, E. Hoare, J. Reynolds, W. Trebilcock, and R. H. C. Gillis and W. R. Coumbe as cox, rowing the gig *Dove* against Polruan and Fowey crews, over a measured mile, recorded the time of 6 minutes and 15 seconds. All the original gigs were built to carry sails in the form of a lug mainsail and a leg of mutton mizzen. On one occasion *Sussex* on an emergency dash from Tresco back to Bryher with the doctor made the 3 mile homeward run in 15 minutes under sail, her stability improved by 5 cwt. of stone ballast picked up on the outward leg from Stony Island.

The gigs sea kindliness is legendary but more of that in later chapters.

Smuggling was a way of life for many around the Cornish Coast and particularly so in the more deserted coves and amongst the Isles of Scilly. In 1828 the Preventive Services stopped the Bryher gig *Venus* from putting to sea because of "smuggling offences" also in 1828 the St. Marys gig *Jolly* was confined to port for smuggling offences.

The Peters built gig *Bull* bought and worked by St. Marys pilots in 1838 met her end with a complete crew returning from a smuggling trip from France. The last sighting of *Bull* was being blown up Smith's Sound under a jury rig in a southerly gale the only remains found was a piece of new wood that had only been fitted the previous day.

Bonnet built by Peters in 1830 for the pilots of St. Martins was probably the gig used by the St. Martins pilot John Nance to make an incredible 25 smuggling trips to Roscoff, a round voyage of about 250 miles. On one occasion after hitting adverse weather conditions, Nance and his crew rode out a storm for 30 hours by just keeping the gigs head to weather.

Finally, according to information given to R. H. C. Gillis by one of Nance's seven daughters (Arabella), James Nance son of John Nance was held on Scilly, on the orders of the Governor Augustus Smith and directed to care for his aged parents and to farm a poor holding on St. Martins, presumably as a penance for his smuggling activities. Records show that on 11-8-1886 Pilots Douglas Skinner and James Nance of St. Martins, for secreting wreck viz: 39 tins of corned beef were fined £10-10 with costs of £1-14-0 or were to serve 1 month imprisonment with hard labour!

Augustus Smith was so determined to put down smuggling that he ordered any cottages built from the proceeds of smuggling to be demolished. As late as 1895 several coastguards were posted in all the Islands, working with the customs to prevent smuggling. It was estimated that in the heyday of smuggling more contraband was landed in Scilly than was at the Customs and Excise warehouse in London.

In 1829 The masters of the gigs *Hope, Champion, Lion, Challenge* and *Defiance* petitioned the Honourable Commissioners of His Majesty George IV's Customs London to repeal the law limiting the crews of any vessels to 4 men only.

Gigs were all banned from carrying 8 oars because the revenue cutters simply could not catch them. If apprehended by a revenue cutter, a gig would simply pull to windward.

The Peters built gigs, also had other uses and came in all shapes and sizes, *Queen* was built by Peters for the St. Martins pilots for

Newquay Harbour in the 1890's in the foreground there are 2 gigs the closer of the two is Teazer the one nearest the ship is Treffy

Newquay Harbour in the 1930s showing the gig Dove on the beach, left hand side of the photo.

salvage work and general carrying she measured 30' 3'' in length x 7' 0'' beam.

Campernell originally built for the St. Ives pilots was bought by the St. Agnes pilots for carrying, she measures 30' 0'' in length x 6' 0'' beam, her stern seat is removable to facilitate the carrying of coffins.

Sussex despite her size 30' 0'' long x 5' 7'' beam (built for the Bryher pilots by Peters in 1886) has won many a race in her time, and in 1929 fulfilled another role, that of wedding transport when she was used to ferry the bride, Bertha Jenkins (a daughter of one of *Sussex's* owners) to her wedding on Tresco.

That brings us on to the other gig uses salvage and rescue of which more in a later chapter, and also racing.

When the Peter's built the first gigs, I imagine they must have been partly an ongoing development of existing boats (it is known that pilotage in the Scillies predates the Peters by probably several centuries) and partly innovation. What the Peters must have come up with was a vessel so novel, fast and sea worthy that every pilot in every port had to have one in order to remain competitive and in business.

This is the only way that the Peters virtual monopoly on gig building can be explained. The life of the pilot was a dog eat dog existence, the first pilot to a ship got the job, inevitably when more than one pilot gig spotted a potential job, a race would ensue in order to get the piloting contract.

Similarly when a new gig arrived the only way to test its performance, was to race it against its opposition. From here it was only logical for the best gig from each port, cove or island to race each other and so it was that gig racing at regattas came into being. In the days before Radio and Television, regattas became venues for mass entertainment. Hayle regatta attracted such vast crowds earlier this century that it became known as the *Henley* of the West. In the early days it was not at all unusual to see Peters built gigs turning up at regattas all over the county, often having been rowed considerable distances to compete and for, given the values of the time, large amounts of money.

In 1861 £11 in prize money was on offer at the Newquay regatta gig race, with Peters built boats taking line honours. 1st *Treffry* £5, 2nd *Dove* £3. At Fowey in 1877 the committee stipulated that only bonefide pilot gigs could race for the £10 in prize money thus Falmouth's *Dido* and Hayle's *Rose* were banned. The race was won by *Annie* of Fowey but two Peter's built gigs *Treffry* and *Dove* took 2nd and 3rd respectively. Also in 1877 at Hayle's regatta *Shah* was brought over from Scilly to win the big cash prizes having then only recently been built in 1873 and being known to St. Ives pilots for whom she was originally built, she was considered to be a crack boat, and did in fact live up to expectations by beating a Hayle crew rowing the St. Ives gig *Branch*, the stroke of the Hayle boat having smashed his oar soon after the start. It was mainly two things that conspired to bring the pilot gigs to an end, the first was the advent of steam powered ships, with there greater manouverability and lack of reliance on the wind as a means of propulsion, the need to take on a pilot became less needed, and finally the 1st World War which resulted in less men to man the gigs as a result of the casualties incurred in the trenches, and a new order in the world. In the years between the two Great Wars many gigs simply rotted away and were burnt as firewood.

Some suffered ignominious ends after glorious careers. At St. Ives *Silver Spray* was burned in a boathouse fire and condemned in 1917. *Branch* was blown off the quay wall in a gale in the 1920's, *Cetawayo* was sold to St. Agnes pilots and simply fell apart after her final race. The St. Marys Gig *A & B* was washed out of her boat house during a gale and smashed to pieces, *Boot* a St. Marys gig just rotted apart and was burnt. *Dolly Varden* a St. Marys gig was cut up and her planks made into a punt. The St. Agnes gig *Daring* was left to rot at Periglis. *Emperor* ended her days at St. Martins – sawn in half and converted into two chicken houses. *Empress* from St. Martins was broken up and used as firewood. *Gleaner*, Peters built, ended her days sawn in two and converted into two punts. *Galatea* from St. Martins was left to rot in the 1930's. *Mistletoe* was left to rot in St. Marys eventually broken up for firewood. *Gypsy* a St. Agnes gig was sold to Padstow and on 27th May, 1964 was burned!

Queen St. Martins gig sold to Truro and later broken up. *Rose* of Hayle was sold to Cadgwith where she met her end under a boulder which fell from the cliff and smashed her. *Sultan* a St. Martins gig was smashed to bits after being washed from her house on Higher Town Beach during a south easterly gale. *Tom Sawyer* a Port Isaac gig ended its life as a grain and fodder bin on a farm. *Zoe Treffry* later named *Teazer* a Newquay gig, she too ended her days as a roof of a chicken house. *Zelda's* stern and bow sections now adorn the wall of a steak bar in St. Marys after she was smashed by a lorry reversing into her on the quay at Padstow in the 1950's.

WHY SO MANY WRECKS ON THE ISLES OF SCILLY?

A Gibson photograph of a gig attending the full rigged 1,128 ton ship Horsa in Bread and Cheese Cove, St. Martins, which went aground on 4th April 1893. The Horsa under the command of Capt. Rolson was homeward bound with a cargo of tinned meat wool and grain. The Horsa was towed off by the paddle steamer Lyonesse only to sink 21 miles south-west of the Bishops Rock. All the crew were saved by the St. Mary's Lifeboat seen alongside in this photograph

Why so many wrecks on the Isles of Scilly?

1. Apart from the obvious reason that Scilly is the first land of any sort for shipping crossing the Atlantic, and lies in shoal ground and is prone to fogs and gales.

It is also in a central position in the worlds largest maritime "motorway" Sir Charles Whitworths "State of Trade" (1776) described the Channel Trade of his day:-

"Down the Channel comes gunpowder, hardwares, woolen manufactures of all kinds, tobacco, spirits, leather goods, fish. Up it came drugs, ivory, wine, sugar, dragons blood, pomegranates, lemons, oranges, gold, diamonds, silk, tea, pepper, coral, cotton, fruits, lambskin, olives, anchovies, gums, aniseed, brimstone, chip hats, beads, oils, soaps, bugles, cochineal, almonds, indigo."

Troutbeck in 1795 could recall seeing instances of 100 coasting sailing ships awaiting favourable winds lying in St. Marys Pool. Obviously with ships from all over the world converging on one spot to either take the English Channel or the Bristol Channel and that spot being beset by contrary tides, bad weather, and shallow reefs . . . then shipwrecks were to be expected. Especially in the days before steam and diesel propulsion.

2. Scilly was a pick up point for pilots and many ships heading for many European ports would call at Scilly to pick up a pilot to take them anywhere from as close as Falmouth to as far as Bremenhaven or wherever. Scilly pilots were famous for their skill and seamanship (though some managed to find the rocks on their own doorstep)! Ships could be coming in for a pilot and then get caught on a lee shore for a variety of reasons, tide, navigational

mistakes, wind and weather, fog etc., darkness, tides and currents etc. etc. or a combination of several of these elements.

3. This cause of wreck was pointed out by R. Heath in 1750 and may have been responsible for many, many wrecks during the latter half of the 17th and first half of the 18th centuries. He quotes Dr. Halley (he of Comet fame) who had noticed that in the contemporary charts and books of navigation that the Lizard and the Isles of Scilly were set east and west of each other, north of 50° of latitude and sometimes as much as 50° 10' latitude whereas their true position is on latitude 49° 55'. At the time when the charts were originally drawn up, this error was corrected by navigators calculating the easterly variation; but when the variation became westerly in 1657 it suddenly became quite significant. No new charts were issued and so ships entering the channel, having missed observations for a day or so and forgetting to allow for variation, would not only fall North of their estimated position and risk running up the Bristol Channel or falling in with the rocks of Scilly, but would have the latter risk enormously increased if they considered that Scilly lay in or above the 50° of latitude.

4. Another reason which pertained then and still exists for ships (and yachts) finding themselves north of their estimated position is the Rennell Current. This current was named after its discoverer Major Rennell in 1793. But its existence had been suspected as far back as 1673. It sets round the Bay of Biscay and then runs North West across the entrance to the English Channel. And after a succession of westerly gales may reach a velocity of one knot. The potential hazard of such a current is obvious and the following examples of wrecks occurring in fog, are direct evidence of its affect on shipping:

(i) when the *Schiller* was wrecked in fog in 1875 she had plotted a course which should have taken her 8 miles to the south of the Bishop Rock.

(ii) The *Earl of Lonsdale* wrecked on 8th June 1855 on St. Agnes was steaming full ahead, the master was sure he was at least 10 miles south of the Bishop.

(iii) The captain of the wooden barque *Independenza* which struck the Crim in fog on 24th September 1881 (and later became a total wreck on The Barrel of Butter, St. Marys) thought he was 15 miles south west of Scilly.

(iv) According to her navigators calculations the *Minnehaha* wrecked in 1910 on Scilly Rock should have passed at least 7 miles south of Bishop light.

(v) The *Susanna* on 14th August 1913 altered her course a point

South "to go *well* clear of the Scillies" and struck the out lying rocks off Annet.

(vi) The *Isabo* struck the Scilly Rock at full speed in 1937 when she was thought to be "13 miles South of the Bishop".

A 75-YEAR-SECRET – *or how the Olympic was nearly wrecked on the 'Stones'*
by John Owen, *The Western Morning News*

The best kept secret of the Cornish seas – the story of how the 46,000-ton White Star liner Olympic was nearly wrecked on the Seven Stones Reef only seven weeks after her sister ship Titanic sank with the loss of 1,500 lives – was revealed yesterday.

The incredible story of a major navigational blunder by a martinet master, Capt. J. H. Haddock, a cousin of Jellicoe of Jutland, was hushed up at the time by horrified White Star Line directors.

They feared public confidence in their ships already reeling after the Titanic disaster, would be totally lost and the line would be doomed.

And the man who has broken the silence of 75 years in the interests of historical accuracy, Mr. Edwin Steel, knows the facts as no one else can since he learned them from his father, Capt. Benjamin Steel, White Star's marine superintendent.

Last night, 82-year-old Mr. Steel spoke to The Western Morning News from his home in the Isle of Wight to tell how the great ship was 40 miles off course, heading for the reef which 55 years later was to claim the supertanker Torrey Canyon.

"They saw the Seven Stones Lightship and they had to take evading action," said Mr. Steel, who believes the liner's engines were thrown to full astern by the startled officer of the watch to halt her rush to disaster.

"All I want to do is to point out that the ship had gone North of the Scillies instead of South."

Why such a mistake was made by a master whose name as a stickler for navigational accuracy was a byword in the line remains unclear. At the internal inquiry which followed the Olympic's arrival at Southampton, Capt. Haddock was said to have admitted the error.

It was left to Cmdr. Lightoller, an officer who survived the Titanic disaster, to suggest a likely explanation years later. He identified a current which, in certain weather conditions, runs very strongly northwards in the approaches to the channel.

Such a current more than 300 years earlier had fooled Adm. Sir Cloudesley Shovell into thinking he was on the French side of the

23

Channel while he was racing full tilt towards the Scillies reefs on which four ships of his Mediterranean Squadron were to founder.

The near miss was to wreck Capt. Haddock's career with equal finality. Although he stayed on with White Star for a short while, he then moved on to obscurity.

"My father had served with him as a junior officer. What Capt. Haddock said was right and that was the trouble – it was as much as an officer dare do in those days to question the master of a ship," said Mr. Steel.

He said Cmdr. Lightoller, without identifying the ship by name, later described the Olympic's escape as "a near shave."

LEGENDS SURROUNDING THE LOSS OF THE ASSOCIATION 1707

On the morning of Wednesday the 22nd October 1707 a fleet of English men-o-war ships under the command of Sir Cloudesley Shovell was approaching the mouth of the English Channel. The fleet which consisted of twelve ships of the line, three lesser rates, a sloop, four fireships and a yacht, had taken part in the siege of Toulon prior to leaving Gibraltar for England on the 29th September.

In the fog and murk of the day and night of the 22nd October. The following ships in the fleet were wrecked.

Phoenix which had been a member of a group of 3 ships which had been sent ahead of the fleet to proceed to Falmouth. Two other ships in the group managed to weather the Scilly Rocks but *Phoenix* struck a rock was holed and was later beached in New Grimsby Channel to prevent her becoming a wreck.

At about 20.00 hours the *Association* in heavy weather in poor visibility struck the Gilstone in the dark and sunk with all hands.

The *Association* was followed by the *St. George* which struck and was then lifted clear by the next wave. The *Eagle* was lost with all hands. The *Romney* lost with all but her quartermaster. The *Firebrand* was also a total loss but her captain and 24 of her crew were saved.

The total loss of life in this catastrophe is not known but estimates range from 1,300-2,000 men!!

The body of Cloudesley Shovell came ashore at Porth Hellick where it was, for a time, buried just above the high tide line. A few days later Cloudesley Shovells body was disinterred and taken to London where, after a state funeral he was reburied in Westminster Abbey.

There are two legends regarding this disaster. One, that Cloudesley Shovell did in fact make it ashore alive and was then set about by a woman who murdered him in his weakened state in order to steal the emerald ring on his finger. The Reverend S. Baring-Gould puts up a very plausible case for one to accept the story as being true his account concludes:

> "That a dying woman confessed the crime to her clergyman and had given the ring to the clergyman saying she had kept it because she feared detection if she tried to sell it. According to Baring-Gould the ring was sent to Lord Dursley, Earl of Berkeley; and from him to one of his descendants Sir George Cranfield Berkeley. It is according to Baring-Gould still in the hands of that family, but has been converted into a locket."

The fact that Cloudesley Shovell's body and that of his greyhound and the bodies of his two stepsons, and that of Edmund Loades, Captain of the Fleet all came ashore on the Island of St. Mary's supports one theory that Sir Cloudesley and his family and friends did succeed in getting away from the *Association* in the Admirals barge only to wreck for a second time close to St. Marys shore.

The other legend which I must add has very little to recommend it other than it is a smashing story goes as follows and comes from Baring-Goulds account, but does have other supporters.

Baring-Gould's account is as follows:

> On the 22nd October, that same fatal day, a sailor, a native of Scilly, venture to approach the admiral and tell him that he was steering to far to the northward and that unless the course of the fleet was changed they could not fail to run her upon the rocks. For this act of insubordination Sir Cloudesley ordered the presumptuous adviser to be hanged at the yard arm of his ship the *Association*, and the only favour granted him, in mitigation of his punishment, was a compliance with the poor fellows request that, before execution of the sentence, he should be allowed to read a portion of the Scripture. The request granted, he read the 109th Psalm in which occur the imprecations: "Let his children be fatherless, and his wife a widow. Let his posterity be destroyed, and in the next generation let his name be clear put out. Because his mind was not to do good, but persecuted the poor helpless man, that he might slay him that was vexed at the heart"

It is known that on the day of the disaster at 1600 hrs. Cloudesley Shovell called his fleet to hove so that soundings could be taken and he could consult with his sailing masters as to their estimated position. All but the sailing master of the *Panther* estimated their position to be in the latitude of Ushant. Cloudesley Shovell concurred with the opinion of the majority.

Baring Gould says that he believes that at this point, a ships lad on board of one of the ships had said that contrary to being just off the coast of France, that the light they thought to be a sail and a ships lanthorn, was in fact the light on one of the Scillies rocks, the Great Smith, and instead of being listened to, the lad was scorned at, sworn at, and ridiculed. This he maintains is the probable source or "small egg out of which so large a fable was hatched forth". He speculates that the lad was probably a Scillonian and that the story was brought ashore by a survivor and his parents or relatives feeling resentment toward Sir Cloudesley Shovell had embellished the facts and in the course of time had "transmuted it from an error of judgement into a crime".

The most probable cause for the *Associations* vague navigation is probably due to a cause that persists to the present day. That of the existence of the Rennell Current. The current which was declared in 1793 by Major Rennell and named after him; had been known of since as early as 1673.

It sets round the Bay of Biscay and then runs north west across the entrance of the Channel and after a succession of Westerly Gales it may reach a velocity of one knot. The potential danger of such a current is obvious and a ship making leeway of 1 knot in fog is in obvious danger.

The main cause for the legend of the hung man aboard the *Association* is this poem written by the Scillonian balladeer and poet Robert Maybee born in St. Mary's 1810 and died in poverty in 1884.

Dark on the Gilstone's rocky shore
The mist came lowering down
And night with all her deepening gloom
Put on her sable crown

From sea a wailing sound is heard
And the seamens shrilly cry,
And booming surge and shrieking birds
Proclaim strange danger nigh

Wrong you steer, Sir Cloudesley, sure
The rocks of Scilly shun;
Northern move, or no sailor here
Will see tomorrow's sun

Hold wretch! Dare tell your Admiral
What dangers to evade?
I'll hang you up on yon yard arm
Before your prayers are said

Oh Admiral, before I die
Let someone read aloud
That one hundred and ninth dread Psalm
To all this sailor crowd

Let it be done, cursed mutineer
As if I know not how
To steer my Association clear
Of every danger now

The Psalm was read, the wretch was hung,
Drear darkness stalked all around
Whilst aloft the dead man swung
Three ships had struck the ground

How sad and awful was the sight
How black and dark the shore
Two Thousand souls went down that night
And ne'er saw daylight more

One man alone of that brave crew
Was saved to tell the tale
How swift and sure God's vengeance came;
He can alone prevail

In truth this wrecking has little to do with the pilot gigs, though they may have been used subsequently on salvage operations, the fact is that it was such a good yard I just couldn't resist including it!!

ANN GLANVILLE THE LEGEND & THE FACTS

Anne Glanville, 1796–1880

1796–1880

ANN GLANVILLE – longshorewoman and oarswoman extra-ordinaire of Saltash.

A. T. Goodman writing in "Devon and Cornwall Notes and queries" Autumn 1988 says of Ann Glanville's influence on women taking part in regattas.

"Within ten years, womens racing at Plymouth regattas moved from being an object of mirth in 1831 to becoming the chief attraction at those regattas in 1841. Saltash women led this change; Ann Glanville led the women.

Ann Glanville is first recorded as a competitor in 1833 when her team was second in a 4 oared gig race at Plymouth. In 1835, at the age of 38, she came in for special praise after her gig *Alarm* had won a race, the reporter adding "she is the glory of Saltash . . . and has added another wreath to her already glowing honours".

In 1838 it was claimed that "in 18 years she has competed in every celebrated local race and has never been beaten". S. Baring-Gould in his book on Notable Cornishmen and Women "Cornish Characters and Strange Events", suggests that Ann Glanville was one of a large family of Saltash riversiders, all of whom were dependant on the Tamar and Lynher rivers for a living and many members were engaged in racing gigs. In 1834 a £20 prize was won by Mary Glanville. Harriet Screech who was a crew member, pulling bow oar in Ann's gig was one of Ann's 14 children. Ann's sons John and George are both recorded as being very big men who used their skills in naval boat races often for wagers involving hundreds of pounds. S. Baring-Gould is mainly guilty of perpetuating the myth that Ann Glanville and her crew of ladies – Harriet Hosking, Jane House,

Amelia Lee and daughter Harriet Screech, did in 1850 travel to the French port of Le Havre on H.M.S. Brunswick and whilst there defeated a crew of French sailors.

Baring-Gould's account of the Saltasher's crew being given a disadvantageous position on the start line and then being roused by Ann Glanville's rallying speech. "Bend your backs to it maidens, and horrah for old England" to overcome the six boats in front of them and eventually take the leading position and win; is probably a load of jingoistic rubbish!!

Ann Glanville and crew did go to Le Havre in 1850 but in a paddle steamer called *Brunswick* not a battleship. The P.S. *Brunswick* sailed from Plymouth to Southampton. From Southampton to Le Havre the Glanville's entourage sailed in another Paddle steamer the P.S. *Grand Turk*.

Once in Le Havre the Glanville crew under Thomas Russell, their coxswain, not Captain Russell R.N. as stated by Baring Gould were, in fact, unable to find French opposition. They did eventually find *a* crew; not the 10 crews stated by the Rev. Baring-Gould, but this was not a crew from the French Navy but one made up of the crew of the paddle steamer *Grand Turk* which, of course, the seasoned oarswomen beat out of sight.

Ann Glanville and her ladies crews, did without doubt, raise a lot of interest in the sport of gig rowing and did row at, and win, at a lot of sporting venues against many male crews. But as A. T. Goodman points out. Ann Glanville was basically a professional sportswoman who hired herself and her crew out to various promoters to row against all comers. The promoters provided publicity and the publicity, not the fact has become legend.

The secret of the Glanville success story was a promoters dream; it was a good scam! It went: "Women are weaker than men, so for a womens crew to challenge a crew of male rowers it looked like an unfair advantage was being given to the men. However if the women were like the Glanvillites, born and bred to the river and highly skilled oarswomen and using a gig built by Mr. Waterman of Anderton, nr. Millbrook, gigs that were famous for their speed and weight it would provide a classic trap for the unwary male punter or amateur crewman.

The basis of Ann Glanville and her female crews success against other female crews was a combination of technique and strength; whilst against male crews it was down to technique, but when matched against other experienced watermen versed in racing skills, the Glanvilles did not always win the day or the race.

Ann Glanville was reported by several sources as having been "presented" to the Queen (Victoria) e.g. Doiges "Illustrated West-country Annual" and S. Baring-Gould. In fact the Fleetwood Regatta where this is supposed to have taken place only had the pleasure of the royal Yachts attendance by virtue of the fact that it was storm bound. The Saltash womens crew rowed about near the Royal Yacht and may have solicited a wave and a nod from their Sovereign.

Their promoter on this tour of the North Country in 1847 was probably a Mr. Green who owned the racing gigs *Viola* and *Nymph* used by the Saltash ladies. He also cox'd for the ladies in their two races at Hull.

Throughout their rowing careers the Saltash *Amazons* as they were often described in the press, constantly courted publicity and pulled a number of stunts in order to achieve this end. After competing in Hull in 1847 they were presented in a music hall type tableau dressed in their rowing kit complete with their gig on the stage of a Hull Theatre.

At Fleetwood the same year they spent two days rowing about Fleetwood harbour challenging "the lords of creation" to race against them.

The account of one of Ann's crew, Jane House, jumping out of the gig is given in several accounts, however, Doige (1886) says it occurred at Newcastle, whereas Doige (1881) omits this detail. Baring-Gould gives this event as happening at Le Havre as do others.

There can be no doubt that Ann Glanville and her crews were paid and professional rowers, they not only had a manager but also a trainer in Mr. Green.

Ann Glanville's successes were compared with those of the Duke of Wellington, and were lauded in all the local newspapers of the day. Perhaps Ann herself was one of her own greatest publicists. In 1851 a reporter asked her whether she intended to enter a skiff race at Saltash for the £1 first prize. Apparently Ann drew herself up to her full height (probably about 6'0") and said "Me pull for a pound, Ann Glanville pull for a pound! She who went over to Le Havre and pulled against the Frenchmen for £20 and beat them out of sight, she pull for a pound! . . . No!" and then her face relaxed into a gentle smile. "I mean to be a lady that day, and tea will be on the table at 6 o'clock."

However, despite the truth and falsehoods it cannot be denied that Ann Glanville made an indellible mark on the sport of rowing and womens rights to participate.

Ann Glanville died on 6th June 1880 aged 84 after a short illness. She was buried at St. Stephens church yard on the 10th June but her impressive funeral went unnoticed by local newspapers.

Ann began competitive racing at the age of 27 and was still engaged in the sport at the age of 51 in the crew of the gig *Chip off the old Block* and that was the most remarkable aspect of this remarkable woman.

In the Reverend S. Baring-Goulds account he attributes the following testimonial to Ann Glanville to a neighbour, and it probably says more about the real Ann Glanville than all the hype and copy she attracted in her eventful life.

"Her was honest to a farthing, clean as a smelt and kind hearted as a queen".

EDWIN TREVASKIS PILOT & COXSWAIN OF THE HAYLE LIFEBOAT

The first Hayle lifeboat Isis. Delivered on station in 1866 and donated by subscription by Oxford University. Hayle's gig launched in 1993 and built by Ralph Bird of Devoran bears the same name

EDWIN TREVASKIS – Pilot and Coxswain of the Hayle Lifeboat

In 1866 the port of Hayle became a lifeboat station when the *Isis* a ten oared, self righting lifeboat, built by Forrestt of Lime house and funded by Oxford University was delivered to the town.

The Coxswain of the lifeboat Edwin Trevaskis, was a man well versed in the moods of St. Ives Bay and further afield. He was one of the old breed of local pilots who as a matter of course would often row many miles in search of a ship to bring to port.

The story is told of Trevaskis, who loved nothing more than to score one over on the pilots of St. Ives, characteristically stealing a march on his rivals on a ship inward bound from Bristol.

It is said that a watch was kept on Trevaskis' gig at Hayle and when it was apparent that it was not about to leave port the St. Ives pilots set off to intercept the ship.

However, when the ship hove into sight the St. Ives pilots were shocked to see the sight of a smiling Edwin Trevaskis at the helm. It would appear that Trevaskis had got to Newquay in another gig and had intercepted the steamer from Bristol at Fistral beach.

The smiling Trevaskis then offered to tow the St. Ives crew back home.

Trevaskis did much of his pilotage work alone, working from a 16 foot gig; his exploits in all weathers and conditions were legendary and he may well have been the coxswain alluded to in A. S. Oliver's "Boats and Boatbuilding in West Cornwall" when he describes the racing record of the St. Michaels Mount gig *Mabel*. He says:- *The Mabel* was raced in many regattas in the under 26' 0" class, she won the Mounts Bay Regatta seven times in eight years. Even the odd defeat, by a Hayle gig, was a greatly disputed race, the Hayle coxswain being accused of assisting his stroke oar.

RACE OF SIX LIFE-BOATS AT PENZANCE.

This picture from the ''Illustrated London News'' shows the Mounts Bay lifeboat race of 1867 it was won by the Sennen boat The Two Cousins Penzance's boat. Richard Lewis was 2nd and Isis from Hayle was 3rd

THE TREDWENS OF PADSTOW

Padstow's gig Teazer built by Peter Foord and Tom Dudley in 1988

The brothers John and Richard Tredwen of Padstow typify the entrepreneurial nature of many of the mid nineteenth century Cornishmen. The brothers John and Richard were multi skilled men who were engaged in a variety of enterprises which included ship and boat building, ship owning, gig owning, salvaging, pilotage and general merchandising. Amongst the many ships built by the Tredwens were the *Mary Seymour* built in 1865 and sunk by U Boat gunfire on 15th June 1916 and the schooner *Cornish Lass* wrecked on Trevellas rocks 6th January, 1896 was 60 tons and launched in 1841.

The Tredwens were not only skilled with their hands, they were also astute business men and were both noted and decorated for their bravery in saving life at sea. In 1833 the ship *Flora* was salvaged by the Tredwens and taken into Padstow for repairs. In 1834 the *Mary* under the command of Captain Carter of Padstow was driven onto the rocks on the River Gannel at Newquay, the ship was salvaged by the Tredwens and taken to their Padstow yard for repairs. November 1836 saw the sinking of the schooner *Catherine* at the entrance to Falmouth harbour. She was raised under the supervision of the Tredwens and taken to St. Mawes after 60 tons of cargo had been dredged from her holds by a Mr. James James of St. Mawes. In 1843 the Cork registered brig *Towan* under the command of Captain Lewis was disabled off Padstow and was in a desperate position. Richard Tredwen using one of his six oared gigs, managed to board the *Towan* and bring her into Padstow harbour where she sank. For this rescue Richard Tredwen and his crew were awarded medals by the Royal Humane Society. Richard Tredwen was again in action in 1845 when he rescued the sole survivor of the wreck of the *William Pitt* disregarding his own safety Richard Tredwen, without any personal safety aids or even the security of a rope, plunged into the roaring breakers to bring the exhausted survivor safely ashore.

On the 8th December 1847 after a period of appalling weather, a large barque was seen at 8.00 a.m. off Newquay. A full gale was howling and the ship, with her sails in tatters and her masts smashed, was in obvious distress. The pilots of Newquay, probably using the gig *Treffry* put out to her assistance. The ship, named *Marchioness of Abercorn* was, however, found to be too dangerous to board in the conditions that prevailed, and the *Marchioness of Abercorn* drove onto Crantock beach at low tide. On Crantock beach four crewmen were rescued by the Rocket Life saving apparatus under the command of Captain Dogherty. Three men drowned when the ships only remaining boat capsized, a gallant attempt at rescue was made by Captain Darke of the schooner *Rose*, Captain Johns of the *Liberty*, and the *Models* mate Mr. John's, and more lives were saved.

By the 17th December two of the bodies had been recovered and 23 members of the crew had boarded the Hayle steamer *Cornwall* bound for Bristol. The *Marchioness of Abercorn* though severely damaged was purchased by the Tredwens and an attempt was made to refloat her, but she leaked so badly that the attempt had to be abandoned. In February of 1848 the Tredwens successfully refloated the ship and she was taken to Padstow for repairs. In August 1848 under the command of Captain Key, the *Marchioness of Abercorn* is recorded as having put into Falmouth for repairs to her main and mizzen topmasts after she had put out on a voyage to Quebec with emigrants.

In 1848 the Tredwens were again in action when they salvaged the brig *Amethyst* which had driven ashore at Porthcothnan. The "Royal Cornwall Gazette" reports that on "January 4th 1850 the schooner *Ocean* under Captain Lewis, which had stranded at Mawgan Porth sometime previously, was got off, again through the efforts of that well known ascientific gentleman, Richard Tredwen Esq." "This" the "Royal Cornwall Gazette" goes on to say is "the third vessel for which he has been successfully engaged during the past two years." The others were the *Mary Ann* refloated from the Gannel Rocks 1833 and the Fowy sloop *Yeomans Glory* laden with iron in 1836.

In January of 1854 the schooner *Sarah*, having missed the entrance to Padstow Harbour, dropped her anchors and spent six hours riding out a tremendous storm outside the Doom Bar. Finally her anchor cables parted and the ship was swept in over the bar. The crew abandoned *Sarah* in the shps boat and all were saved by the timely assistance of Tredwen's gig and crew.

in 1857 Richard Tredwen moved to Newquay, his house "Eothen" has long since been demolished, but the site is that of the small park of the same name overlooking the beach. In the same year, 1857, Richard Tredwen also took over the shipyard at Newquay harbour. In 1859 the Padstow gigs *Storm* and *Arrow* built and owned by the Tredwens were both involved in the rescue and salvage of the S. S. *African* when her engines failed off Padstow. The *African* grounded on the Doom Bar. The Tredwen's gigs successfully got pilots aboard both vessels and a rescue plan for the *African* was rapidly put into operation. The *African* was warped into the safety of Hawkers Cove by a large shore party and the services of Mr. Gregor Chapman's team of oxen. Awards of £2,800 were eventually made, £300 going to Tredwens for the services provided by the shore crew and gigs and £2,500 going to the *Queen*, the Hayle based steamer which had originally taken the *African* in tow off Padstow.

On the 20th of March 1869 a gale from the north drove many ships scurrying into the shelter of Padstow. The *Sarah Williams* from Port Madoc, bound for Trieste with a cargo of slates, drove into Polzeath. Her crew all waded ashore at low tide. About a mile away a dismal fate befell the St. Ives schooner *Bristol*; she was lost with all hands under Pentire. Whilst out at sea, the *Slaven* of Ragusa, under the command of Antonio Fiscovech and en route for Falmouth from Odessa with a cargo of maize for Gloucester, was in distress under the Great Mouls Island, off Pentire. With three anchors down and her pumps choked by maize the crew had been dissuaded from a suicidal attempt at rowing across the Doom Bar by the local pilot, David Volk (who later drowned on the *Minnehaha* wrecking at Scilly in 1874). The *Slaven* continued to pitch and soar at anchor and all the time the levels of water in her holds rose by a steady inch an hour, and she continued to make undecipherable signals. Captain Hicks of Wadebridge declared he could decipher the *Slavens* signals if a copy of Marryatts signal book could be located. A horseman was sent at the gallop to Polzeath to see if the master of the stranded *Sarah Williams* had one, he did not, so the rider dashed on to Padstow. He finally returned triumphantly with a Marryatts only to find it was the wrong volume! The gloom of evening was fast falling when at last the *Slavens* signal was deciphered; it read "Send a lifeboat as soon as possible"!!

The coastguards signalled to Volk and the Austrian crew to row ashore, but on Volk's advice the crew remained aboard. The crowd assembled at the scene dispersed when the coastguards refused to use the Port Isaac gig. Then suddenly the *Slaven* dragged her anchors and carried on into a rocky creek under Pentire where Volk and the crew remained until after the gale had moderated. Both the *Slaven* and the *Sarah Williams* were salvaged by gigs from Tredwen's yard assisted by the Cardiff tug *Advance*.

The Tredwens were famed not only locally but much further afield for their salvaging expertise and were engaged on many salvage contracts all over the County and Country for many years from the mid to late 1800's. This brief account is only a brief listing of their activities, which would probably, if fully researched, provide enough material for a book in its own right (or write).

AUGUSTUS SMITH AND THE PILOTS OF SCILLY

The coxswain of the gig Bonnet urging his crew on

One evening in 1834 when the weekly mail cutter *Lord Wellington* had berthed in St. Mary's Pier a man stepped ashore who was to become, at first reviled, hated and despised but later was to become respected and even loved. This man was Augustus John Smith a gentleman from Hertfordshire who had taken up the lease of all the Islands of Scilly on a tenure based on 3 lives.

He went on to establish himself as the Justice of the Peace, Chairman of the Council and Lord Proprietor of all Scilly. He was to be regarded as "Lord of the Isles".

At the time of his arrival the Islands had suffered many years of mismanagement and abuse by those in charge and poverty was widespread on the off Islands. Augustus Smith tackled all the many problems in an autocratic, dictatorial fashion, many, at the time, hated Augustus Smith and his Rules, but later had to concede that what he did, had worked.

Under Augustus Smith education became compulsory for all children, 30 years before it did so on the mainland. The school curriculum of the time covered navigation for boys and net making for girls.

Augustus Smith always had a special affection for the Scillonian pilots and following the laws passed on 1st October 1808 which superceded the old "Court of twelve" system in which a dozen of the Islands most respected citizens decided not only the laws but also selected the men who were to become *Scilly Pilots*. Under the new system all the pilotage, including that in the Islands, passed to the jurisdiction of the Bretheren of Trinity House. Trinity House did not have any comprehension of the peculiarities and special circumstances which applied to the Islands and only made allowances for eleven licensed pilots to cover all the Islands. To make things even worse all these were chosen from St. Mary's. In 1808 there were 23 Pilots on St. Mary's alone; 18 on Tresco, 14 on St. Agnes, 14 more on St. Martins and 8 on Bryher, needless to say there was a riot, but even after this the Bretheren of Trinity House only upped their numbers to 37 licences.

The ensuing years became farcial with many if not all the pilots continuing to work as pilots whether they were licensed by Trinity House or not.

Legally there were now two classes of pilot, the official Trinity House approved and licenced pilot and the unlicenced unapproved "hoveller". Scilly had become a compulsory pilotage port and all ships had to take on a pilot and under the new system a Trinity House Pilot was superior to all others. Inevitably this class system caused trouble off and on but when Augustus Smith came to the Islands he decided he would resolve the problem. He told the unlicenced pilots to carry on and threatened any Trinity House pilot with eviction if they challenged his decision. Augustus Smith even solicited the help of Mr. St. Aubyn the M.P. for West Cornwall to bring the matter to the House of Commons, and in his will, he left one pilot, James Jenkins of Bryher, who he felt had been particularly hard done by, a sum of £300 for "his great distress caused by Trinity House refusing to grant a renewal of licences".

The unlicenced pilots did continue in the Islands largely as a result of Augustus Smith's patronage in 1848 there were, it has been estimated, at least 200 men sailing as pilots out of various ports and coves of the Isles of Scilly out of whom only 37 were officially licenced by Trinity House.

It may be interesting to note that the one and only Trinity House Pilotage Certificate to cover the entire British Isles was granted to a Scillonian, Captain Ashford. As steam power superceded sail the number of pilots licenced and unlicenced dwindled, from the early 1800's (when as many as 300 ships are recorded as having visited Scilly in one day) up until 1876 the number of Trinity House licenced pilots remained at 37 or thereabouts. In 1876 the number was more than halved at 15, in 1900 the figure again dropped by almost half to 8, 1915 saw the figure drop to 5, by 1958 only 3 licences were issued and in 1961 only one pilot remained on the Trinity House lists along with a provisional pilot.

CONSTRUCTION DETAILS

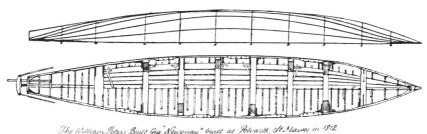

The William Peters Built Gig "Newquay" built at Polwarth, St Mawes in 1812
Still in use and owned in trust by Newquay Rowing Club

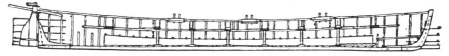

- Cornish pilot gigs are traditionally made from small leaf elm. However, in 1953 when the Newquay gig *Dove* was refitted Frank Peters discovered that she had been built of broad leaf elm.
- *Newquay* was examined in 1955 by Mr. Brabyn of Padstow and apart from other defects he found the iron bolts in the oak keel had rusted to the size of matchsticks. Iron and oak are not a good mixture, oak when wet produces an acidic solution which virtually disolves iron. Old time ship wrights who built the luggers always used trenails when fastening oak. Some builders used just oak trenails, others used one trenail to one iron fastening. Trenails were often used because of the superstitions which abounded. One of which was the old theory that somewhere at sea was a huge magnetic rock or field that would draw out all the fastenings of a ship as it passed over it. The other was that iron fastenings would adversely affect the compass.
- Stretchers ship into notches attached to margin planks screwed to the timbers, these also support the moveable ceiling or bottom boards.
- Since garboard and sheer planks lie nearly flat they were made 4½″ including the laps. Whereas on the turn of the bilge where there is maximum curvature, plank widths were reduced to 3½″.
- On Treffry the keel camber or rocker is about 4″ the keel line is not straight but rises in a gradual curve as it moves aft.
- Keel dimensions are given as:
  John Gardiner 3½″ x 1¾″
  Edgar J. March 3½″ x 2″
- Planking dimensions are given as:
  Harold Kimber) 5/16″

John Gardiner) 5/16"
Edgar J. March ¼"
Alf Jenkins ⅜"

- Thwarts fit the skin snugly as do the hanging and lodging knees.
- The undersides of the lodging knees are not notched to seat on the risings.
- At the end of each thwart there are two hanging knees called thwart knees.
- All thwarts except the bow thwart and the steering seat were fitted underneath with a pillar support. The pillar fitted into a special pad fastened to the centre platt and notched into a U shaped housing under the thwart.
- Built to weigh a little under 7 hundredweight so they could be lifted to be launched or carried ashore by their crews without too much effort.
- In the Peters time all joints were given a liberal application of whale oil applied with a feather according to Frank Peters.
- All driven copper nails were ragged or notched i.e. had barbs cut in them with a chisel before being driven. The nail then resembling the barbs on a fish hook.
- No hog pieces were fitted and the triangular rabbet into which the garboards fitted was only ⅜" deep, the planks being skew nailed. The garboard fitted in the rebate and was caulked with cotton.
- Thwarts were usually about ¾" thick and supported by a central pillar which gives the boat tension and the thwarts an upward curve. Without the pillars fitted the gigs become limp and would leak in the bilge planking.
- Iron nails were used in the old boats to fasten the keels as it was felt that copper would stress and weaken with the constant flexing.
- In many of the older gigs the stern is higher than the bow.
  Newquays stern is 3' 0½" high her bow is 2' 11"
  Dove stern is 3' 0" high her bow is 2' 10½"
  Sussex stern is 3' 1" high her bow is 2' 11"
- Inside height from top of keel to gunwales in the lowest part of the gigs waist:
  Newquay = 22½"
  Dove = 22"
- The rounded stem was made up of three pieces of timber to keep the grain as true as possible.
- The after deadwood was fitted, joining the stern post to the keel, the stern post was also let into the keel and secured by a ½" horizontal wooden dowel.

Oak or American Rock Elm was used for gigs keels, it was incidentally rock elm imports that introduced the dread "Dutch Elm Disease" to our shores, which led to the loss of all the mature Elms in the country.

Rowlocks are never used on gigs to prevent damage to the gig, if they were used and a rower missed a stroke or "caught a crab" it would do immense damage to the ¼" planking. Whereas a similar accident using thole pins would usually be limited to the loss of only the thole pin.

BOW SIDE

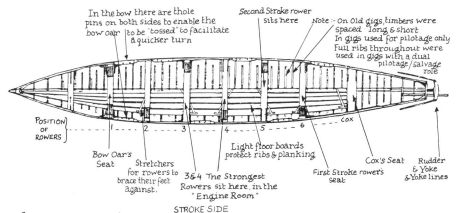

In the bow there are thole pins on both sides to enable the bow oar to be "tossed" to facilitate a quicker turn

Second Stroke rower sits here

Note :- On Old gigs, timbers were spaced "long & short" In gigs used for pilotage only Full ribs throughout were used in gigs with a dual pilotage/salvage role

POSITION OF ROWERS — 1 — 2 — 3 — 4 — 5 — 6 — COX

Bow Oar's Seat

Stretchers for rowers to brace their feet against.

3 & 4 The Strongest Rowers sit here, in the "Engine Room"

Light floor boards protect ribs & planking

First Stroke rower's seat

Cox's Seat

Rudder & Yoke & Yoke lines

STROKE SIDE

Gigs are of various sizes but modern gigs, usually copies of "Treffry" are about 32' long and no wider than 4'10" at its widest point. The hulls must be planked in Cornish Small Leaf Elm.
Gigs are built to weigh about 7cwt.
The old oars or sweeps were usually made of ash and would measure up to 18'0"
Modern paddles are of silver spruce and differ in size according to the position in the gig ie. stroke & bow oars being shorter because of the gigs narrow shape in these positions

The old St Agnes gig "Gipsy", renamed "Gypsy" when sold to Padstow Regatta Club in 1955 for £60. Had the distinction of being the last gig used for pilotage The date of this pilotage was Dec. 21st 1938, the ship "SS. Foremost" the pilot~ Jack Hicks of St Agnes, Isles of Scilly, and the fee £3 · 65 pence.
"Gipsy", the last gig built by Samuel Tiddy was burnt on 27-05-64 following her destruction when a lorry reversed into her on Padstow quay.
Richard Gillis salvaged her rudder pintle which was later used on the gig "Newquay"..

These line drawings and notes were taken from John Gardner's book "More Building Classic Small Craft" many gigs have been built from these plans, both in Cornwall and the U.S.A. The lines and measurements were taken from Newquay Rowing Club's gig "Treffry" by Harold "Kim" Kimber. The "Treffry" was built by William Peters of St. Mawes in 1838 for the Treffry Company. She was and is considered to be William Peters finest creation. After a major refit in 1989 Treffry seems all set for another 151 years

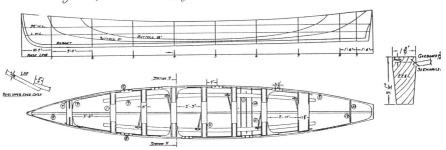

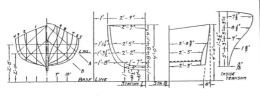

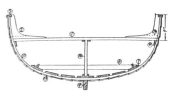

TYPICAL PILOT GIG DETAILS FROM NOTES BY HAROLD KIMBER AND PHOTOGRAPHS

1. THWARTS ELM ⅝" THICK. BOWED SLIGHTLY UPWARD BY PASS.
2. HANGING OR THWART KNEES NATURAL CROOKS. 2 TO A THWART.
3. LODGING KNEES AGAINST INSIDE OF PLANK, ON TOP OF PART AND FASTENED TO IT.
4. RISER 9" BELOW SHEER GENERALLY. 11½ STATION 6, 7½ AFTER THWART
5. GUNWALE MOLDED 1½ SLIGHT TAPER AT ENDS ¾" THICK.
6. STRETCHERS LET INTO CLEATS FASTENED TO THE MARGIN STRIPS.
7. MARGIN STRIPS SCREWED TO THE TIMBERS.
8. THOLE PIN PADS BORED WITH TWO 1-INCH HOLES 4½" ON CENTERS.
9. KEEL SIDED 1⅝" MOLDED 3¼".
10. TIMBERS ⅝" x ⅞" TAPERED TO ⅝" x ⅜" AT HEAD, FITTED OVER LANDS. 6" ON CENTERS.
11. ALTERNATE TIMBERS END JUST BELOW RISINGS.
12. CROSS BRACE HOLED TO TAKE END OF BOOMKIN FOR SAILING RIG.
13. PLANKING 12 STRAKES CORNISH NARROW-LEAF ELM ½" THICK.
14. FILLER PIECE BETWEEN THWART KNEES.
15. 1" DIA. HOLES 4½" ON CENTERS FOR THOLE PINS.
16. REMOVABLE PAD FORCED UNDER THWART TO GIVE SLIGHT HEATED BOW.

OFFSETS: FEET, INCHES, EIGHTHS TO INSIDE OF PLANK

	STATIONS	1	2	3	4	5	6	7	8	9	TRAN.
HEIGHTS ABOVE BASE LINE	SHEER	3-9-0	3-5-1	3-2-2	3-1-2	3-1-0	3-1-6	3-4-0	3-8-0	3-9-7	4-0-0
	RABBET	1-1-2	1-0-7	1-0-7	1-1-0	1-1-4	1-2-1	1-3-1	1-3-7	1-4-4	1-4-6
	BOTTOM KEEL	0-10-0	0-9-5	0-9-5	0-9-6	0-10-2	0-10-7	0-11-5	1-0-5	1-1-1	1-1-4
	9" BUTTOCK	3-0-4	1-6-7	1-3-2	1-2-7	1-2-7	1-0-4	1-7-0	2-3-4	3-2-1	
	18" BUTTOCK		2-6-5	1-7-7	1-5-5	1-4-7	1-7-0	2-2-0			
HALF-BREADTHS	SHEER	0-9-6	1-7-7	2-1-5	2-4-0	2-4-1	2-3-0	1-11-0	1-3-2	0-11-4	0-7-4
	32" W.L.	0-8-1	1-6-3	2-0-7	2-3-2	2-3-5	2-2-0	1-9-2	0-11-5	0-6-1	0-0-5
	LOAD W.L.	0-5-1	1-2-2	1-9-4	2-1-0	2-1-3	1-10-5	1-4-3	0-6-2	0-2-7	0-0-5
	KEEL	0-0-7	0-0-7	0-0-7	0-0-7	0-0-7	0-0-7	0-0-7	0-0-7	0-0-7	0-0-5
DIAG-ONALS	DIAGONAL A	1-0-7	2-0-4	2-7-3	2-10-5	2-10-7	2-8-5	2-3-5	1-5-7	0-4-7	0-0-0
	DIAGONAL B	0-10-0	1-6-6	2-0-3	2-2-4	2-2-6	2-0-5	1-7-7	0-11-7	0-6-7	0-0-5

DIAG. A 4' ABOVE BASE LINE, OUT 2'-3" ON L.W.L. DIAG B 3' ABOVE B.L. OUT 1'-2" ON L.W.L.

56

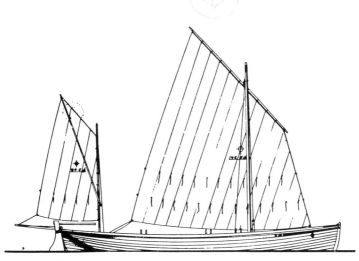

The St. Michaels Mount Gig "Mabel"

'Mabel' was built on the Mount by Burt in 1867. She was built for Lord St. Levan. Dimensions :- 24'0" x 5'5" x 1'11½" (inside). Spar Dimensions :- Foremast 16'-18' x 3" dia. Foreyard 12' x 1½"-2" dia. Mizzenmast 11'-12' x 1½" dia. Sprit boom 10' x 1½" dia. Mizzenboom 4' x 1½" dia. Sail Areas - Foresail 142·5 square feet. Mizzen sail 36·5 square feet. Total Sail Area 179 square feet.

P.J. Oke who took the original drawings noted that the sails in this drawing of the Mabel were drawn proportionately from the larger sails of the 28'0" gig "Sally" -

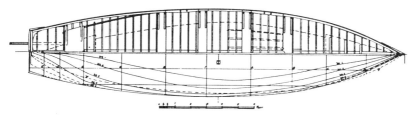

The dimensions and position of the bottom boards were not available when P.J. Oke took his lines but they are indicated in the above drawing by the dotted lines. The hull colour is given as white, with one red strake below the rubbing band. Inside the gig is painted white from gunwhale to the thwarts and red below. When measured by Oke in 1937, the 'Mabel' had been found to have twisted out of shape longitudinally. The stem was found to be approximately 3" out of centre

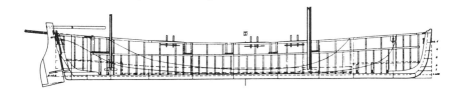

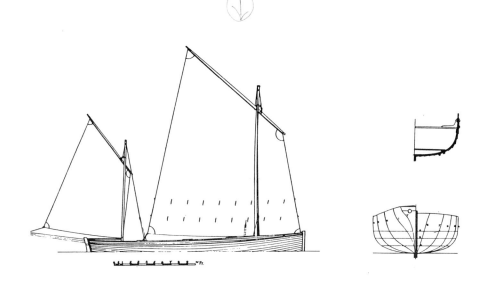

The St. Ives Gig Type, this basic shape survived well into
recent times, albeit adapted to take an inboard engine.
This type of gig was designed and used as a fishing
boat usually crewed by 2 men and a boy there was
a large fleet of these, usually carvel built boats in
many Cornish ports, fishing for mackerel or pilchards.
This example drawn by P.J. Oke in 1935 was 26'6½" L.O.A
6'4" BEAM x 2'6" DRAUGHT. her foremast was 20' x 4' dia tapering
to 2¾", the foreyard was 16' x 3", the mizzenmast was 13'6" x 3" dia
tapering to 2". Oars were of ash and measured 14' to 16'

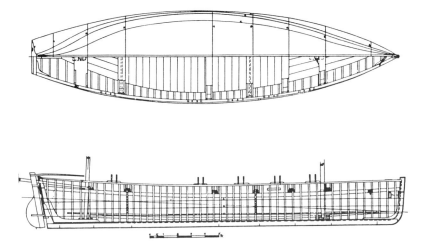

- The stern post was usually of the same materials as the keel and of the same dimensions.
- Cuts were made in the stern post and the stem to carry the keel rebate through and to take the ends of the planking.
- The after edge of the stern post was cut away to take the 1″ thick transom and all was lined up with the rebates.
- The moulds were fitted after the stem and stern were rivetted to the keel. The planking then commenced in the style of traditional clinker build.
- Strakes were kept as long as possible without joins, strakes were only given one scarf and all scarfs were staggered throughout the gig.
- The fastenings were all copper roves and nails rivetted on the inside nailing was at three inch spacing.
- Timbers were steamed and bent into position, they were then marked to coincide with the plank lands and the notches were cut to joggle the timbers to the planking, the timbers were then re-steamed and then fitted to the hull.
- Gunwales on the originals were of solid construction. Thole pins were always used, rowlocks were never used.
- Stretchers were fitted at an angle for the rower to put his foot against. These stretchers were bars of wood that could be lifted and moved fore and aft, usually to three different positions, in a specially made block fastened to the higher bilge bottom board.
- The planks lap or lands were ¾″ and only the top edges are bevelled.
- There are no solid floors, only bent frames and half frames.
  Scantling – dimensions given by Edgar J. March.
  Keel – American Elm sided 2″ moulded 3½″
  Stem 3″ x 1½″ tapering to ½″
  height about 3 foot, some gigs 2″ less, other ¾″ more.
  Stern post 1″ thick, 20″ high, 3½″ wide at heel, tapering to nothing at the head.
  Inner Post 1⅜″ x 1¼″
  Dead wood 1¼″ thick
  Planking ¼″ thick
  Timbers ½″ wide x ½″ thick to ¼″ at thinnest section
  Golden Eagle ⅝″ thick x ⅝″ wide
  In gigs for pilotage timbers were alternately positioned 1 long and 1 short spaced at 6″ centres.
  In gigs for salvage work all timbers were long.
  Thwarts 5½″ wide x ¾″ thick some chamfered at the edges.

Knees fitted were	Standing	lodging
1st thwart	1	1 on aft side
2nd thwart	2	2 fore and aft
3rd thwart	2	
4th thwart	2	1 of aft side
5th thwart	2	
6th thwart	2	
7th thwart	2	1 on aft side
8th thwart wider	2	

- Distance between thwarts 28" – *Czars* spaced at 27¼"
- Oar placings – Bow, number 3, and number 5 oars to port number 2, number 4 and stroke oar to starboard. Facility for thole pins on both sides of the bow oar to enable the oars to be tossed to the other side to speed the rounding of a mark.
- The thwart knees are filled in on the side that the rower sits.
- The gunwales are strengthened by a grown oak breast hook fitted inside the stem head and a grown oak knee connecting the inside of the transom of the gunwales aft. No other supports or stiffenings were added.
- Port Starboard and central bottom boards were fitted in and locked in place by the central plank fitting over a couple of copper eyes fitted to the keel and protruding up through slots in the boards through these protruding eyes simple wedges securely hold the boards in place.
- The stern boards or stern platt is made up with a removable central section to enable the bung to be fitted and removed without the need to remove the complete platt.
- On the mainland the bow and stern platts are respectively called the bow and stern sheets.
- On the outside of the gig all that is fitted, except the stem and keel bands is a rubbing strake and a bilge rubbing piece.
- The rubbing strake in fitted to the second sheer strake right up snug against the sheer strakes lower edge.
- The bilge rubbing piece is a 7-10 foot piece of elm fitted on the run of the bilge and tapered so as to reduce water resistance and drag.
- The rudder is made of elm and attached by means of pintles and gudgeons one of each on the rudder and their opposites on the stern.
- The rudders double piece was always fitted to the starboard side only so as not to foul against the mizzen outrigger when the helm was "hard a port".

FISHING FLEET, ST. IVES.

61

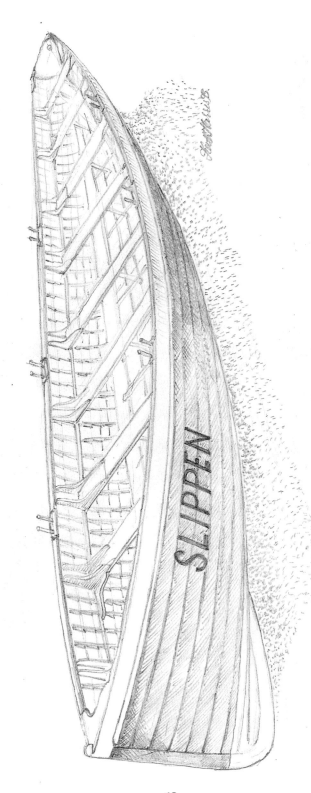

- The rudder is steered by a yoke and yoke lines, however in some of the old carrying and large salvage gigs a short tiller was sometimes used, enabling the cox or helmsman to sit right aft and thus provide more room for cargo.
- Gigs were fitted with mooring rings on the stem and stern posts, and tack hooks for attaching the tack of the lug sail, and main sheet hooks also for use when rigged for sailing. All these metal fittings were in non ferrous metal i.e. bronze or brass.
- The rig of gigs was always a dipping lug mainsail but whilst a dipping lug mizzen was usual, a variety of rigs were used on the mizzen.

  Some used a boom fastened to the mizzen mast with a gooseneck the sheet was then led aboard from about half way up the boom, between the steering yokes and was made fast to the mooring ring.

  The most widely used rig was to fit an outrigger through a hole in the transom through the port side of the stern post the inboard end fitting into the outrigger step. The outrigger could then be used as the lead for either the mizzen boom or if the sail was loose footed as a lead for the sails clew.

  The "leg of mutton" or lug sail was then hoisted on the leeward side of the unstayed mast with the halyards acting as a stay on the windward side, the tack having been clipped (if the lug rig was used) to the hook on the inside of the weather gunwale.

  A few boats also used the sprit sail rig on the mizzen, where a spar is used from the tack to the peak of the sail, the loose footed sail being sheeted from the clew via the outrigger.
- There were usually four sets of reef points on the sails.
- The hoist on the mainsail was attached to a traveller with a strop attached to the gaff.

AN ACCOUNT OF WRECKS & RESCUES INVOLVING PILOT GIGS AROUND THE CORNISH COAST & AMONGST THE ISLES OF SCILLY 1666 TO 1955

The Bryher gig Czar photographed by Gibsons receiving cattle from the wreck of the Minnehaha in 1910

1666

Ye Shippe Royall Oacke, wrecked on the *Bishopp*, crew rescued by St. Marys gigs. The ship was wrecked on January 18th, the crew cut, bruised and tattered were rescued 52 hours later on 20th January.

1700

Two St. Agnes pilots drowned when their pilot boat overturned trying to save a shipwrecked crew stranded for days on a rock.

During a violent storm a vessel was lost on the Isles of Scilly. Many of the crew were drowned, but some scrambled ashore where they remained several days, till at length, a St. Agnes pilot boat got out to them, but the boat capsized and nearly all were drowned including two of the pilot boats crew before *Woodley*.

1745

The *Boscawen* had been the French frigate *Medee* until she was captured by Lord Boscawen and renamed after himself in 1744. In October 1745 the privateer (as she now was) *Boscawen* under the command of Commodore George Walker was under a great deal of strain in all kinds of ways. Her light build was designed for speed and manouverability not the huge weight of extra guns and ammunition that Walker had loaded on to her. This added burden resulted in many leaks as she laboured home from the Azores. Then the main yard having been incorrectly fastened, parted from its slings and crashed onto the deck, adding damage and stress to the hull. The crew were near mutinous and exhausted, the ship a floating wreck and without her anchors when she drove into St. Ives Bay on 24th November 1745. Awash, and too deep in the water to enter St. Ives. With all distress signals flying and cannons booming the Boscawen tried to heave to, outside the harbour but was soon driven ashore. Due to the gallant rescues effected by both townsfolk and the boatmen, boats, gigs and their crews only four lives were lost in this incident which could have easily been a total disaster.

1779

Nine Scillonian pilots drowned leaving seven widows and twenty eight children.

1782

On the 13th August 1782 the Venetian vessel *Providentia Divina* with an exotic cargo of Castile soap, wine, almonds and oil drove onto the Crim and was wrecked drowning two of the crew. A St. Agnes boat which had put out to her assistance found and rescued eleven men they found afloat on a raft. Other boats from the Islands also came out to the wreck. Three more survivors were blown into New Grimsby Harbour clinging to the ships mast.

1784

4th March, 1784 a transport making for Scilly during a strong south west gale reported to pilots that she had spoken with a packet ship from India about an hour previously and which they now feared had gone aground. Several gigs made a search and eventually found the wreckage of a ship on Rosevear in the Western Rocks which proved to be the *Nancy*, a packet from Madras. There were no survivors. An actress, Mrs. Cargill, reputedly carrying a small fortune was one of the three bodies removed from the wreck. The others mostly those of army officers returning from India were too putrified to be removed and were left to the sea.

1788

On 10th December 1788 a boat going from St. Marys to Tresco was lost drowning nine men, all of whom had large families.

1789

The *London* bound for London from Carolina went ashore on the Western Rocks on 25th April 1789 and was totally wrecked, none of her cargo of indigo, rice and tobacco was salvaged but a great deal of money was found scattered on nearby rocks. One survivor Joseph Tuttle, carpenter, was saved, but the boats were only able to reach him after he had spent nine days stranded on a rock by huge seas.

1790

Tradition or legend has it that in this year a Peters built gig was delivered to Padstow as a lifeboat, the cost being met by a member of the Clergy. Also the year Peters began building gigs at Polvarth.

1790

The derelict *Elizabeth* with her deck gone but some masts and rigging alongside was taken in tow by some Island boats but was later cast adrift, she eventually smashed to pieces on the Norrad Rocks.

1791

St. Marys Pilot boat lost between Penninnis Head and the Gilstone on 4th April 1791. Eleven men were drowned, one survivor died half an hour after he was rescued.

1798

The *Collossus* an English man of war of 74 guns was lost on 10th December 1798 whilst on a voyage from Lisbon for England all but one of her crew was saved by Islanders. The man lost was the quartermaster Richard King who fell overboard whilst taking soundings. The *Morning Herald* Wednesday 19th December 1798 states that the Islanders "at very great risk, exerted themselves to the utmost in their cutters and open boats".

1799

In the Royal Institute of Cornwall Journal 1992 there is an account of the "Journal of John Pollard of Newlyn 1794-95" edited by P. A. S. Pool, the entry for 28th December 1799 is as follows:-

> "Hevey gall wind, two breges and three pilot boats hove on shore, 2 brigs and one pilot boat lost, one breg laden with fish the other with freute, at the same time John Pollard was onbord *Rachall* pilot boat being one of the three wich was hove onshore"

1801

23rd January, John Pollard of Newlyn recorded that he and fifteen men "received for the salvage of the ship *Princes Roiall* £1000".

The Legend of the tragedy of the Men of Samson

1801 is the date which is given most credence for the following incident. It is said that the men of Samson left their island to aid a ship in difficulties off Broad Sound in the Western Rocks, some three or four sea miles from Samson. When the pilots boarded the vessel they were "Surrendered to" by a crew of ten French Privateers who had recently captured the ship and were in the process of taking her to France when they found themselves in the Western Rocks.

The Samson men took the ship into St. Mary's where they received instructions to take the ship and their prisoners to the Royal Navy at Devonport. Whilst on passage to deliver their prize and their prisoners it is said that the ship struck the Wolf Rock and the Samson crew of nineteen men and boys, the entire male population of the little Island and the ten privateers were all drowned. It would seem unlikely that a crew of pilots from the Scillies would shipwreck on a rock so close to home as the Wolf which lies roughly midway between the Isles and Lands End. What actually happened we shall never know. It is easy to speculate, did the ship incur some damage whilst in the Western Rocks which developed with tragic results on the voyage from St. Marys to Devonport? Did the French Prisoners retake the ship? Even the date is a mystery. Alf Jenkins, a Scillonian author of several books on Scilly gigs, says that, in his research, he was unable to find an exact date for the disaster. A former school teacher and author, Mrs. Tiddy, was similarly unable to find an exact date. However, Alf Jenkins did find in the course of his research, some old rent books for Samson, and found that in 1715 the islands were inhabited by only twelve people, and thinks that these were the twelve women forcibly removed from Samson because of the hardship of living on Samson without any menfolk. There were no payments in the rent books for 1774 and it was 1800 before people were living on the island again and were recorded as having paid rent. 1801 could be the date however as it is 35 years later in 1836 when the Samson men are again in the record books as being official pilots. On the 13th December 1838 thirteen men of Samson, seven Woodcocks, six Webbers bought the cutter *Fly* from St. Agnes pilots. *Fly* was 36' 9" L.O.A. x 11' 0½" Beam x 7' 5" Draft., 18 Tons and was first registered in St. Agnes in 1815. It was certainly unlucky thirteen for the Samson men, as on 2nd December the following year *Fly* broke free from her moorings drove ashore and was totally wrecked. After five more years of scrimping and saving, on the 10th February 1842 the Samson men purchased another cutter, this time by four Woodcocks and two Webbers. The cutter they bought was another St. Agnes boat called the *Defiance*, built at St. Marys, she measured 37' 0" L.O.A. x 12' 5" Beam x 7' 7" Draft, and was first registered at St. Agnes in 1826. Tragically this venture was also doomed to failure, two years later on 5th November 1844 *Defiance* also came ashore after dragging her mooring and was destroyed. The Webbers and Woodcocks remained on the Isle of Samson for only another eleven years. After they finally left, the island has never again been populated except by the birds and holiday visitors.

1802
March 1802 – A large eight oared boat was carried three miles overland (presumably from Hayle) and other boats came out from Hayle in an attempt to save lives from the East India man *Suffolk* driven on shore at Gwithian. The *Suffolk* had been at sea for six months on a voyage from Bengal to London, her crew was starving and laid low with scurvy.

1802
The brig *Fortune* of Banff Scotland sailing for Dublin from London struck the Seven Stones reef. The crew were all rescued by a passing vessel, a Yarmouth brig, and safely landed at Scilly. However the wreck of the *Fortune* was discovered by the crew of a Scillonian pilot boat who boarded her. Of the four pilots to go aboard only two escaped with their lives when the ship suddenly and without warning sank under them.

1803
On 28th November seven men were drowned in an attempt to board a Batavian Ship which was in distress off St. Ives Island. She had been captured by a small privateer/cutter from Polperro, and taken to St. Ives, the cargo had been valued at £90,000 when it was taken aboard in Batavia. They were only a short way from the pier when heavy seas capsized their gig.

1804
The *Active* sailing from Portsmouth to Chepstow in ballast was lost in an easterly gale on the 24th December 1804, the crew was saved by Scilly pilots.

1805
The armed Prussian galliot *Bacchus* of and from Emden sailing for Guernsey with empty barrels had somehow managed to find her way on to the North Cornish Coast, she was salvaged by the pilots of Padstow on 12th January 1805.

1810
A November gale caused the eventual wrecking of the *Harriet and John* on St. Agnes. The crew were all saved by pilots. When the weather finally abated they also managed to salvage her cargo.

1814
Four pilots put out to an anchored brig off Padstow in what was described as a "Tempestuous sea" they all drowned when their gig capsized. One of them was to have been married the following day.

1815
Four men from Tresco who put out to salvage some floating wreckage were drowned 14th January 1815.

1815
Early on the morning of 3rd July 1815 a crippled schooner severely damaged after an encounter with a privateer a few weeks previously, floundered her way along the coast from Tol Pedn to Porthgwarra. Off Porthgwarra the crew abandoned ship and rowed off to a nearby brig. Seizing their opportunity a group of local fishermen launched a gig with the aim of salvaging the abandoned ship. As they rowed off toward the schooner their intentions became clear to the original crew who had by this time been picked up by the nearby brig. Despite their shouts and warnings, the three men from the gig went aboard, only minutes later the ship suddenly turned over and sank, taking the three would be salvors to their deaths.

1815
Two Bryher pilots, C. Jackson and James Tregarthen, were drowned whilst attempting a rescue. James Tregarthen had just returned home to Scilly after serving the past 8½ years in a French prison. The wrecked ship was the West Indian brig *Queen Charlotte* of Glasgow. Though having lost two of its crew, the gigs remaining crew, stuck to its task, and eventually saved fourteen lives. A subscription list for the two drowned men received £100 from Lloyds and £50 from the Duke of Leeds.

1816
When attending the Welsh sloop *Ant* of Swansea three of Padstows pilots and the *Ants* mate were drowned.

1816
Mary of Liverpool returning from Rio De Janeiro to Liverpool wrecked

in the Scillies, seven of fifteen men aboard an attending gig were drowned. Ultimately the ship was a total loss but her crew was saved.

1817
On 7th December 1817 the Custom house boat and a pilot boat sank on their moorings off St. Marys.

1818
Padstow pilots braved enormous seas to save the crew of the Irish butter schooner *Eliza Jane* which wrecked at Trebetherick 24th February 1818. An hour later the Newhaven sloop *Mary Ann* also returning from Ireland was wrecked right alongside and her crew of six was also rescued.

1818
A Scillonian gig from Old Town with the oars double banked, capsized in a rough sea between Penninnis Head and the Gilstone rock after cox Tregarthen broached the gig. Seven men were drowned, seven were rescued by a Pilot cutter from Agnes.

1821
Three crew of the St. Marys gig *Horse* were drowned when returning from putting a pilot aboard a ship. The wreckage of *Horse* was washed ashore at St. Marys the next day (21st May 1821).

1821
The Old Town gig, the gig with no name, whilst putting a pilot aboard a ship near the Gilstone off Penninis she filled with a sea and six men were drowned.

1825
The *John and Ann* bound for London from Cadiz with a cargo of wine was blown onto the lee shore of Bryher. The pilots managed to get pilot William Jenkins aboard but the *John and Ann* failed to weather the entrance to New Grimsby Channel and was lost with all hands including William Jenkins.

1825
Boats from St. Marys brought in the *James* of North Shields with a cargo of wood.

1825
In a full north easterly gale the snow rigged *New Braganza* loaded with

oats and bound for Shoreham from Dublin was boarded by Padstow pilots led by William Hibley and brought to safety on 25th October, 1825.

1826

In a similar mission to that undertaken on the *New Braganza* the pilots of Padstow again braved the perils of the Doom Bar to go to the assistance of the relatively new snow rigged ship *Lord Dupplin* recently launched in Perth. The gig tragically capsized in its attempt to reach the ship and three men were drowned. The Snow's crew were then saved, after heroic action and tremendous seamanship, by a pilot cutter which on approaching the shore was also capsized, although all on board did manage to struggle ashore.

1826

The French ship *Ocean* which had put into St. Ives earlier for expensive and extensive repairs and was afloat outside the harbour awaiting a fair wind to sail. In the ensuing gale she parted her cables and drove onto Hayle Bar. The pilots of Hayle and St. Ives who had come to the crews aid at the greatest risk to their own lives, were in direct contrast to the nearby villagers, who flocked to the wreck site intent on plundering the wreckage and got exceedingly drunk in the process.

January 1827

A brig at anchor in St. Marys pool, Isles of Scilly on 12th January 1827 was much damaged and a pilot boat was smashed to bits on the rocks.

October 1827

On the 29th October the Tresco gig *Hope* saved all the crew, except one black seaman, of the schooner *Susan* of Boston.

November 1827

The Royal Cornwall Gazette 10th November 1827 reported the American Ship *Susanna* laden with cotton and logwood as having struck and sunk on the Seven Stones reef on 2nd November 1827. All the crew except one was saved by a Tresco pilot boat. The *Susan* and *Susanah* are probably the same ship!!

1827

The Danish Galliot *Tvende Sodskende* sailing from Bilbao to Copenhagen sprang a leak and sank four miles off Bryher, the crew was saved by a pilot boat and landed in Scilly.

74

1828

When the brig *Sarah* came ashore on rocks near Flushing the local inhabitants must have thought back to the disaster of the Transport ship *Queen* which drove ashore in a gale in 1814 and wrecked herself totally on Trefusis point in less than half an hour with a loss of 330 lives. At the wreck of the *Sarah* the villagers of Flushing burnt furse and tar barrels to illuminate the scene as masts were felled and cut free and victims were hauled ashore in an empty barrel. Lloyds agent William Broad was awarded the R.N.L.I. Gold medal for his initiative in saving eleven lives by means of an open boat. It was Lloyds Agent William Broad who in 1812 sold the Peters gig *Newquay* to the Newquay Pilots.

1828

On the 7th December 1828 the South Sea whaler *Phoenix* was lost on the Stones reef off Praa Sands. *Phoenix* was only a fortnight out of the Thames and should have been voyaging south on a three year voyage. Instead she was fighting for her life in Mounts Bay. The *Phoenix* had been damaged in a gale west of the Isles of Scilly and with topmasts down, had turned and run before the storm making for shelter and repair in Falmouth. In thick fog the *Phoenix* became embayed and at 4 a.m. on 7th December struck the Stones reef off Praa Sands. The crew took to the boats, two seamen and four apprentices made it to seaward whereas the mate and seven men who tried to row ashore were capsized in the surf and but for the bravery of eight seamen of Helston who plunged into the surf and pulled them out, they would have perished along with the *Phoenix's* master, Captain Phillips, his 1st Officer and thirteen crewmen who perished when the whaler crashed onto the beach and was pounded to pieces. Those off shore were later rescued in mountainous seas by a gig manned by coast-guards, pilots and fishermen.

1828

Five men out of a crew of eight were lost from a pilot gig on Golden Ball Bar.

1828

May 1828 Mr. Richard Pearce, the Lloyds agent, put Manbys inshore rescue apparatus and his own six oared gigs to good use in saving the master and five crewmen of the brig *Albion* of Plymouth, which had been driven ashore to the east of Newlyn in a heavy gale. In 1851 Mr. Richard Pearce was awarded a silver Medal by the National

Institution for the Preservation of Life from Shipwreck for his repeated services in saving life from shipwreck.

1830

A small boat (possibly a gig) going from St. Marys to Tresco much over loaded shipped a heavy sea and sank. Five out of the fourteen on board lost their lives and some of those saved were resuscitated only with the greatest difficulty. The survivors included the Rev. James Law, Minister of Tresco, and Mr. James the school master.

1830

The gigs *Blucher*, *Dove*, and *Champion* assisted in the rescue of the crew from the 390 ton Dutch Barque *Borodino* on the 7th March 1830. The *Borodino* was en route for Milford Docks from Sierra Leone and had two Scillonian pilots on board when she wrecked on Carn Marvel. The *Borodino* was carrying a cargo of oil, oak, ivory and gold dust. All twenty one on board were saved including pilots for Scilly and Milford.

1830

27th September 1830 the gig *Hope* returning from St. Marys shipped a heavy sea and sank, five of the fourteen aboard perished.

1833

The Brig *Thomas* of Fowey running before a north west gale into St. Marys struck Woodcocks Ledge and sunk in seven fathoms of water, the St. Marys pilots launched a gig and saved all of the crew. Four months later she was raised and beached June, 1833.

1833

A St. Martins gig with ten men aboard put out to attend a brig flying a pilot pennant on 21st January 1833. However in huge seas she was capsized and sunk immediately, six of her crew were lost.

1833

Bonnet is first mentioned by name when she was at the scene of a shipwreck, this may have been the wreck of the *Joseph*, the ship sunk near the Seven Stones, but the crew was saved.

1833

The Royal naval Brigantine *Forester* 10 guns bound for Africa from Plymouth and the large East Indiaman *Providence* bound for Bombay from London had both run ashore. *Forester* on St. Martins and

Providence on Crow bar. A pilot boat attempting to render assistance to H.M.S. *Forester* was driven ashore and wrecked. The *Forester* was towed off by a steam tug ten days later. The *Providence* was patched and floated off but she capsized and was eventually sold as a wreck.

1835

On September 10th 1835 a large Brixham schooner was wrecked leaving with slate from Mr. Averys Delabole Quarry. In the attempt to rescue her crew, marooned on a rock at Portgaverne, a pilot gig capsized drowning Thomas Apps, Abraham Masters and Diggory Stroutt.

1836

The gigs *Juno* and *Unicorn* and the coastguard boat assisted the pilot cutter *Ranger* in rescuing the crew of the brig *Edward Charlton* wrecked on Bartholomew Ledges 20th December 1836.

1836

On 4th February the gig *Champion* and the pilot cutter *Cyclops* (master Obediah Hicks) rescued the crew of the *Fame* which was later abandoned. The *Fame* eventually washed ashore with its pig iron cargo on St. Agnes. The cutter *Cyclops* was sold to Augustus Smith in 1837 and was broken up and used as fencing.

1837

Captain Mitchell Brown Wade of the brig *Dewdrop* received the R.N.L.I. Silver Medal when he coxed the Padstow Harbour Associations largest gig, using a steering sweep at the rescue of crews off Padstow, following the collision and wrecking of the Jersey Apple Smack *Britannia* and the Welsh schooner *Jane*.

1838

The *Royal* Bude lifeboat became reality after King William IV's attention was drawn to the lack of life saving facilities on this part of the coast which had claimed so many vessels in recent years, including the Bude pilot boat. He decreed that money from the Duchy coffers would be set aside towards a lifeboat for Bude.

1838

The Porthcressa based gig *Juno*, the ill fated gig *Bull* and the St. Marys gig *Bee* based at Pendreathen (*Bee* and *Bull* were almost brand new having been just built by Peters of St. Mawes that year) attended the wreck of the schooner *Victoria* ashore on Crow Bar 15th February

1838. The *Bee* actually capsized during the rescue but survived unscathed as did all her crew. The *Bull* Peters built at St. Mawes in 1838 met her end on a smuggling trip to France, she was last seen sailing in a southerly gale in Smith Sound under a jury rig. The only remains of this gig was a piece of wood only fitted the previous day by a member of the crew who did not sail on this fated trip because his wife was about to give birth. *Bull* vanished in Smith Sound between Annet and St. Agnes.

1838

On Christmas Eve 1838 the schooner *Rival* drove ashore outside the safety of the harbour wall at St. Ives. The local pilots responded immediately by launching three of their gigs but failed to get any one of them through the pounding surf to effect a rescue. The Manby rescue apparatus was brought to the scene but several attempts to get a line aboard were also unsuccessful. Still undeterred the fishermen launched two pilchard seine boats but to no avail these were carried too far to leeward and beached on Porthminster, fortunately without any loss of life. Eventually the pilots made another attempt using the gig *Rasper* and were within a few yards of the *Rival* when the gig was swamped by a huge sea, half full of water and totally unmanageable the gig was driven ashore and finally capsized near Pednolver rocks, again without any loss of life.

A local seine owner S. F. Cocking volunteered the services of his pilchard tow boats and one was quickly manned and launched. The tow boat did manage to get a line aboard the *Rival* but before it could be secured it too was washed to leeward of the ship. The tow boats crew gallantly bent to their oars for a second attempt, only to be overwhelmed by a tremendous seas which washed two oarsmen from their benches and drove the tow boat in total disarray, minus a number of oars, onto the beach. Again miraculously all hands on the would be rescue boat were saved. It was now about four o'clock in the afternoon with daylight beginning to fail and the storm and tempest still raging. Yet still more men stepped forward and another mission was begun, again using the tow boat, it again got tantalisingly close before being beaten back. Finally the pilots decided on one last attempt and relaunched a gig. This time their efforts were crowned with success and they managed to safely rescue the *Rival*'s crew of five and land them on Porthminster beach. They also later managed to get the schooner off the rocks and into the safety of the harbour. The Shipwreck Society later awarded a total of five silver medals to the main participants in this rescue.

1838

On the 17th April the 312 ton London registered brig *Neptune* bound for Rotterdam from Liverpool drove under Godrevy Lodge in a North North Westerly gale. She was so utterly smashed to pieces that the coastguards could only identify her when her longboat containing her ships papers and the name of her captain, Daniel Grant were washed ashore. Her cargo which had been salvaged from the beaches of Hayle and Gwithian was sold days later. The *Neptune* had been launched 27 years earlier in 1811 and had been refitted in 1830. The ships crew including the captains 14 year old son are buried in Gwithian churchyard, their grave marked by a single stone by the tower. One of the ghost stories told goes:- that on the previous evening the St. Ives pilots had gone out to a brig off St. Ives Island, as they came under her bows one of the pilots stood to grab the bowsprit chains. As he grabbed the chains, the whole ship, just disappeared.

1838

On the morning of 18th November 1838 the Indiaman *Larkins* hove to off the Scillies to take on a pilot. No sooner had pilot Hicks stepped aboard then the *Larkins* was felt to strike heavily three times, then, leaking badly she floated clear. Pumping began at once but the pumping was not keeping apace with the incoming water. Captain Ingram his passengers, and the mails transferred to the pilot cutter leaving the *Larkins* to the care of her crew. When Captain Ingram reached Penzance he recruited a fifty strong crew and went in search of his ship. After a hunt of the Western Approaches from the Lizard to the Wolf which lasted for twenty four hours, Captain Ingram and his crew returned to Penzance. Captain Ingram then travelled to Falmouth and consulted with the authorities there, finally Captain Plumridge ordered the wooden paddle steamer *H.M.S. Meteor* to go in search of the *Larkins*. The missing ship was finally located off the Manacles, having been taken in hand by pilot James of Coverack who had brought twenty six local men to man the pumps, he was heading for Falmouth. Pilot James and his crew managed to get the *Larkins* safely into Falmouth and save the majority of her cargo which included silks, indigo and saltpetre.

1839

In either March or April the Plymouth Schooner *Solace* Barrett master, bound for her home port from Lisbon, struck Rosevear in fog and was wrecked but all hands were saved. The following day (the 28th March or April) a St. Agnes gig engaged in salvage was capsized in heavy seas near the wreck and her crew narrowly escaped drowning.

1839

Gigs from Scilly picked up large quantities of American deal wood in late January indicating that a ship had been wrecked.

1839

In the early hours of the morning of 22nd February," 1839, the St. Agnes pilot gigs were alerted to the likelihood of a wreck amongst the Western Rocks. The local boats went out and found the remains of the 165 ton brig *Louissa Hannah* of Poole which had driven ashore on the Ranneys with the loss of her entire crew.

Of the huge amount of oranges and lemons, the cargo of the brig, and many casks of wine only twenty five kegs of wine and a small amount of fruit were ever recovered. Papers found nearby revealed the name of the ship and her master, H. Moores, and that she was homeward bound from Lisbon. She became a total loss.

1840

On 19th November, 1840, an amazing tale of shipwreck rescue and survival unfolded on Porth Hellick beach when the St. Marys Islanders discovered the derelict hulk of a capsized brig on the beach. The *Nerina* had sailed from her home port, Dunkirk, on the 31st October with a cargo of sail canvas and oil. The 114 ton brig had a crew of seven including the captains 14 year old nephew, Nicholas Nissen. On the morning of 16th November the *Nerina* encountered a severe gale off the Scillies and was forced to hove to, in order to reduce sail. When down to storm canvas she was struck by and knocked down by a huge sea and completely capsized. In the process, one of her crew, a seaman called Bourneard was lost overboard. Whilst inside the forecastle two other crewmen Vincent and Vantire were able to grab the windlass bits and haul themselves to safety. A third seaman, Jeanne Marie, became ensnared in a web of tangled ropes and was drowned after a desperate fight for life. Inside the inverted hull the cargo had crashed down and this enabled Vincent and Vantire to scramble over the cargo and work themselves toward the sound of the voices of the ships master, Captain Everaert, and the mate Jean Gallo and young Nicholas Nissen. Eventually all four men and the boy were together in the inverted ships cabin. In this cramped space, lit only by the light filtering in through the cabin skylight, they were forced to crouch in the freezing cold, immersed waist deep in water, unable to stand and only able to stretch to relieve cramped and frozen limbs by taking turns. The five endured two days in this hell hole with no food or water, with the air becoming increasingly foul and with only the bark bindings on the oil casks to chew on for sustenence,

80

their situation was desperate to say the least. The mate began to chip away at the hull with his deck knife in the hope of making a hole; if his knife had not broken and he had succeeded, they would have surely perished, it was only the airtight hull that was keeping them afloat!

The foul weather continued and on the night of Wednesday 18th November the capsized hull was being alternatively hurled and plunged into the sea, when the seaman Vincent lost his hold and footing and fell through the cabin hatch and drowned. The remaining foursome desperately scrambled towards the bow and soon noticed that the water level had begun to drop. Shortly after, they noticed rocks and it became clear that the ship had drifted ashore. About 7 a.m. on the 19th November an Islander found the brig high and dry. Approaching the hull he pushed his hand through a hole he discovered in the ships side and was terrified when it was siezed and held fast from inside. Eventually he was released and raised the alarm and local farmers descended on the wreck and hacked the hull open to liberate the survivors who had, by this time, been trapped inside for three days and nights.

It was later discovered that the *Nerina* had been sighted drifting about a mile offshore, the previous day. The gigs which went out to investigate had abandoned their attempts to tow the wreck in when their tow ropes had broken repeatedly in the heavy seas. Had they not made this attempt there can be little doubt that the *Nerina* would have been taken out to sea on the ebbing tide and would have been lost.

1841

On 21st November 1841 the Port Isaac gig went out to the 400 ton barque *Cassandra* of Newcastle loaded with Newcastle coal the *Cassandra* was at the mercy of the elements having lost her rudder, she was without steerage and wallowing helplessly before a north westerly gale between Port Isaac and Boscastle. The Port Isaac gig crew could not reach her in time and the *Cassandra* drove in under Beeny Cliff with the loss of all hands.

1841

A figure head attributed to *Neptune* in Tresco Abbey gardens is really that of *Thames*. On 4th January 1841 the 500 ton packet steamer *Thames* en route for London from Liffy ran into such heavy seas off the Isles of Scilly that her boiler room soon became so flooded that her boiler fires were extinguished. Sail was set but to no avail, the *Thames* with eleven cabin passengers, thirty new recruits for the British Army and a crew of twenty five was soon standing into danger off the Western Rocks. Within a short time the ship was driven onto Jackies Rock. Aboard the ship, flares were burnt all night but were not seen until day break. The St. Agnes gig *Thomas* with a crew of ten put out first followed by *Bee* and *Briton* and as the tide made they were followed by the 45 foot half decked pilot cutter *Active*. These were to be followed by the St. Marys lifeboat which was delayed because of problems in mustering a crew, this was the only recorded service by this lifeboat (which was of the Plenty type 26 ft. long, pulling ten oars it was built in Newbury, Berkshire in 1828). The gig *Thomas* was the first to arrive at the scene of the wreck only to find the *Thames* with her bows under water and the survivors cowering on the poop deck. The *Thomas* neared the wreck with waves crashing about her and in danger of being swept either onto the rocks or the wreck at any moment and managed to get a line aboard. The gigs crew began to get the women aboard; a woman called Celia Morris had to be prised from her fathers arms, but she was first aboard the *Thomas*. When the *Thomas's* crew had Celia Morris aboard a huge wave crashed over the top of the wreck and swamped the gig, while half the crew frantically baled to keep the gig afloat the other half were struggling to rescue two more ladies (Mary Naylor and May Gregory) by this time the seas were breaking over the wreck so frequently that the *Thomas* could not be maintained on station without the very real danger of being totally demolished by the raging seas. The *Thomas's* crew then decided to row to Gorregan where they could transfer the three women to the cutter *Active* The huge seas now running prevented any attempts to get close to the *Thames*, but the gigs stayed in the lee of Gorregan waiting for the conditions to improve or the gale to abate. Aboard the wreck an attempt was made to launch the ships lifeboats, both were smashed to pieces before they reached the water. Panic set in and an attempt was made to launch a raft, it capsized hurling all five of its occupants into the sea, only one of whom (Edward Kearon) made it to the safety of the rocks. He was found the following morning fast asleep amongst some of his drowned colleagues. Of the three women rescued by the St. Agnes gig *Thomas*, one account says they all died aboard the cutter *Active*, the trauma and exposure had been too much for them, another says they were landed at 3 p.m. at St. Agnes. Depending on what account you read between 57 and 65 persons are said to have perished. The Institution awarded a Gold Medal to Charles Steel coxwain of the lifeboat and silver medals to the first four volunteers whilst monetary awards went to the rest of the crew and to the crews of the gigs and the cutter. The lifeboat was not used again and in 1855 the station was closed.

1842

The Brisons, twin slate peaks that jut out of the sea near Cape Cornwall, mark the site of the wreck of the schooner *St. Austell*. Bound for Penzance from Newport with coal. Her crew launched her longboat, which promptly capsized. A passing schooner ignored the crews plight and by the time the Cape Cornwall gig had arrived Captain Tellum had been swept away.

1842

On 23rd October 1842 on a dark and gale wracked early morning, a Newcastle West Indiaman named *Bosphorus* bound from Glasgow for Jamaica struggled into the roads. A pilot gig was hurriedly launched but the high surf immediately hurled it back onto the beach. In the loom of the pierhead light and a blazing tar barrel which constituted the St. Ives harbours leading lights, the gallant pilots stripped to britches and waistcoats, emptied the gig and launched her again. After an hour long struggle they managed to board the ship and though almost exhausted, and probably beginning to suffer from exposure, they first helped to safely anchor the ship and then as the tide rose, they sailed her to Hayle where they almost had another mishap; the ship having almost stranded on the Hayle Bar on the way in.

1843

Bristol schooner *Pearl* rescued in similar way to *Bosphorus* on 18th February 1843, and on 26th February the brig *Euphemia* was also warped in by St. Ives pilots after her captain had been swept overboard and lost.

1843

The brig *Towan* of Cork was disabled and in a perilous state off Padstow, Richard Tredwen of Padstow boarded her from a six oared gig and got her into Padstow harbour before she finally sank. Tredwen and crew were all awarded medals by the Royal Humane Society.

1844

The Dutch barque *Niekerie* of Rotterdam sailing from Samarang and Batavia for her home port with a cargo of coffee and sugar was wrecked on the Western Rocks at 1.00 a.m. on 21st February. Of her complement of nineteen only the sailmaker Simon Grieve and a seaman Christian Soupe were saved. They were rescued from Rosevear on the morning of the following day, a highly skilled rescue carried out at great risk because of the tremendous seas that were running.

1845

In May 1845 at Port Isaac a young man called James Rounseval was celebrating his luck. He had just inherited a sizeable fortune and was out with three friends on an expedition to shoot sea birds, on the way back they called into Port Isaac and proceeded to get very drunk and instead of taking the advice offered by the local boatmen to take on some ballast, they took on even more beer. Then the inevitable accident happened, their slightly ballasted boat capsized. The Port Isaac gigs rushed to save the floundering drunks but were too late to save Rounseval, who, with his pockets full of lead shot, went down like a stone, as did one of his friends.

1845

The Yarmouth schooner *Lady Anne* with a cargo of railway iron struck the Ridge on 20th January 1845 during a north westerly gale. St. Ives pilots went to her assistance. She was anchored and dragged almost on to Pedn Olva and it was evening before the exhausted pilots and crew got her alongside Smeatons pier where she promptly sank.

1845

The 275 ton snow *William Pitt* was lost under Trebetherick, where she was pounded to pieces in minutes. Only able seaman James Hewson was saved, he was hauled from the surf by Padstow pilot, gig owner and shipwright/salvor Richard Tredwen. The *William Pitt* was bound for Gloucester from Alexandria with a cargo of horse beans.

1847

On December the 8th 1847 a large barque was seen at 8.00 a.m. off the coast of Newquay, the weather had been blowing hard since the end of November and 8th December was no exception. A full gale was blowing and the barque *Marchioness of Abercorn* bound for London from Quebec with a cargo of deal was in serious trouble, her masts broken, her sails in shreds. The *Marchioness of Abercorn* under the Command of Captain Edgert and registered in Londonderry had met with one gale after another on this voyage and as a result of damage incurred on her transatlantic passage she had been diverted to Cork for repairs and Captain Edgert's original crew had deserted.

The Newquay pilots launched a six oared gig probably the *Treffry* in an attempt to render assistance. However, they failed in their attempt and the 1,300 ton barque was soon driven ashore on Crantock beach. See chapter on Tredwens of Padstow.

1849

The French vessel *Victor Joules* of Nantes with a cargo of flour was found abandoned near the Seven Stones and was brought into New Grimsby by two pilot boats, she was later sold by auction.

1951

The Scicillian brig *San Georgio* sailing for Hamburg with a cargo of olive oil struck the Crim, came off, filled with water and capsized. The crew abandoned ship and were rescued by the *Galway Ark* who landed them in Scilly. The derelict ship was eventually located and towed back to St. Marys by a collection of eleven pilot boats and five other vessels. The *San Georgio* was repaired and sailed again as *The Lion*, E. Odger master.

1852

With a cargo that included rum, lime juice, pimentos, sugar, ebony, coconuts and fustic, the wooden barque *Mary Hay* bound for London from Jamaica was entering Broad Sound from the Northwest on the 13th April, 1852. The Scillonian pilot on board was pointing out the many dangerous rocks in the area to the master on the way in. He had scarcely started to eat his meal down below when the *Mary Hay* crashed onto the Steeple rock and began to sink.

Eventually the 225 ton *Mary Hay* was anchored near Samson. After many hours of work at the pumps the *Mary Hay* suddenly lurched over onto her side, narrowly avoiding falling onto the gigs and boats alongside and without any loss of life. Some of the cargo was salvaged but the ship was sold along with some remnants of her cargo for £72 and floated to St. Marys some days later and broken up. The figure head of the *Mary Hay* is in the Valhalla museum.

1853

A gig from Carter's yard Padstow rescued the crew of the *Providence* of Exeter after she had sprung a leak and sunk on the Doom Bar.

1854

Whilst running before a northerly gale two schooners making for the shelter of St. Ives harbour grounded on the sandbank off Pednolver point. The *Swift* of Exeter bound from Newport to Sheerness with a cargo of iron struck first, only to be followed by the *Concord* of Looe bound from Neath for Southampton with a cargo of Welsh coal. Both vessels were on the same bank with the *Swift* slightly more inshore than *Concord* had the tide been on the way in rather than ebbing, as it was, both ships would have without doubt been pounded to pieces there and then. However, the position of the crews on their stranded ships was not an enviable one, surf and spray pounded both schooners relentlessly. The *Swift's* crews had taken to her bowsprit whilst the more vulnerable *Concord's* crew had taken to the rigging. An attempt at rescue involving a pilchard seine boat was unsuccessful, the seine boat belonging to Bolitho and Hitchens was driven back. The pilots then launched a six oared gig and managed not only to reach but also rescue the crew of six aboard the *Swift* and bring them ashore. The next trip out to the *Concord* proved more difficult, the gig being in too great a danger in the surf around the ship. Bolitho and Kitchen's seine boat was again launched along with a boat belonging to the Cornwall Company, these were accompanied by two gigs who would assist should the pilchard boats be swamped. After a tremendous struggle the seine boats managed to get under the *Concords* bow and the crew on the fore mast were got off. Unfortunately the *Concords* captain who had climbed the main rigging was washed overboard and lost whilst trying to get to the ships forecastle and safety. As a mark of respect and gratitude for the rescuers bravery a public subscription for the four boats crews raised £152.90. This incident occurred on 20th December 1854.

1854

Richard Tredwen and his crew made a brave rescue of the crew of the *Sarah* a schooner which had come to grief after her anchors parted on the Doom Bar.

1859

The Padstow gigs *Storm* and *Arrow* built by the brothers Richard and John Tredwen (who were both involved in many salvages all around the Cornish coast) were both involved in the salvage of the S.S. *African* when her engines failed off Padstow. She was towed to Stepper Point by the Hayle steamer *Queen*. When they began to enter the approaches to Padstow the *African* struck the Doom Bar, although the *African* did not get swept broadside to the waves, the waves began to sweep over her quarter. The Tredwens seeing the danger and one suspects having a good eye for business, using *Storm* and *Arrow* managed to get pilots aboard both vessels and the gig *Arrow* was then able to get a warp from *African* to a capstan inside Stepper Point where a large shore party eventually warped her into the safety of Hawkers Cove. £300 in salvage was awarded, £110 for the services of the shore crew and £190 for the services of the gigs *Arrow* and *Storm*. Whilst the steamer *Queen* was awarded £2,500. Even a team of oxen were pressed into service on this rescue owned by Mr. Gregor Chapman of Lelizzick

(who stood by with an axe in case the *African* ran amok and he had to sever the ox traces.)

1861

The American ship *Award* wrecked on Gweal Island off Bryher was on her maiden voyage from the Bristol Channel in ballast when the elements and then disaster overtook her. Such was the ferocity of the storm that the Bryher men were unable to launch. During the next 24 hour period on the wreck, the *Awards* foremast was knocked over by the waves. Fortunately the mast fell onto the rocks and the crew of the *Award* were able to crawl from the disintegrating wreck to the comparitive safety of the island where they remained for a further 24 hour period until the weather had abated enough for the Bryher pilots to rescue them. Out of the money awarded to the Bryher men for their rescue of the *Award* came the £32 that financed the building of the gig *Golden Eagle* named after the Golden Eagles on the reverse of the gold dollar pieces that they were rewarded with. *Golden Eagle* was originally built with a beam of 5′ 2″ but she was "pulled home" to 4′ 10″. The salvage/rescue money for the *Award* was £100 paid in golden dollars.

"The Award from Liverpool did sail
Bound for New Orleans
She struck upon the rock of Gweal
And went to Smithereens"

1861

In a severe gale, one that drove in and tormented the ships anchored and moored in Penzance before the harbour, the basin and lock gates were erected. The Polacca brig *Hero* of Bideford was torn free from the mooring that she shared with two other windbound ships the *John* of Bideford and the *George* of St. Ives. *Hero* had put into St. Ives suffering from storm damage to her fore mast incurred on her voyage from Newport to Plymouth with coal. It had occurred that *Hero* was on a buoy mooring with the two other ships and during the evening the wind again got up to gale force from the south south west, *Hero's* captain, Captain Forlwer had gone aboard to check the moornings but at 10.30 the three ships all broke free at the same time. Whereas *John* and *George* both managed to sail into, and beach safely in the harbour *Hero* swung out into the harbour mouth and into danger. A pilot gig came to the *Hero's* assistance but their offer of help was refused by Captain Fowler, two of *John's* crew went on board to lend a hand, but the situation got more dire. Captain Fowler hailed the gig to take a hawser back to the buoy but it parted, a second rope was not long enough, and then the gig became disabled. Two local men aboard *Hero* returned to their own boat and advised Captain Fowler and his crew to join them before it was too late. They agreed but instead of just leaving, they wasted time collecting personal belongings, and by the time they did abandon, it was too late they had lost the relative shelter of the pier and the *Hero's* boat capsized drowning the Captain, three of his crew and the two helpers from *John*.

1862

The shallow waters to the South of St. Martins known as the flats saved a ship on the 24th January, 1862. The Cardiff owned brig *Alexandrine* having been abandoned by her crew in the roadstead, was boarded and brought onto safety of the flats by the local pilots who received a £97 reward from the *Alexandrines* grateful owners.

1865

On 22nd September 1865 the brig *Ceredig* struck the Western Rocks was attended by gigs and eventually saved.

1866

There was a widespread fear on the mainland that spread to Scilly that Bolitho's Bank in Penzance was about to go the way of many other provincial, private banks i.e. to the wall. Many Islanders had money banked with Mr. Bolitho and a number of them in the panic to save what they could chartered the gigs of the Islands to row to Penzance so they would be able to draw out what money they had. As the group neared the bank (Now Barclays) Mr. Bolitho, who had been tipped off, greeted the group. He assured them that all was well with his bank, and opened the tills to show they were all full of bank notes. He managed to convince the deputation so well, that when they left the bank for home, not one had closed an account, or removed any money.

1867

When on passage from St. Ives to Lands End or vice versa it is always a temptation to pass between the Brisons and the mainland, I have seen the local boats working gear and motoring through the gap but, myself, I have always erred on the side of caution in both small fishing vessels and yachts. On the 31st March 1867 the 1,192 ton full rigged ship *Hamlyn* set sail from the Thames in ballast bound for Cardiff. The voyage had been beset by gales which had necessitated taking shelter in both Torbay and Plymouth Sound. On the evening of the 18th April, 1867 *Hamlyn* was making a fair speed across Mounts Bay at 9 p.m. the Longships were sighted and pilot Birchfield set a course to clear Cape Cornwall. However during the period of time that the master, Lefevre, and mate Napleton Beaver were down below, the helmsman swung the ship off course and before pilot Birchfield had a chance to correct matters the *Hamlyn* had crashed onto the Bridges reef at an estimated eight knots or more. The crew all took to the boats and were all saved but the *Hamlyn* did not fare so well. A Sennen gig was launched with the intent of investigating the possibility of salvaging her, but to no avail, the two men from the gig who managed to board the *Hamlyn* were soon driven back and the ship entered her death throes; within an hour she began to break up, and an hour after that her masts all fell and the bows were torn off, by dawn on the 20th April she had gone without trace.

1868
A French Brig the *Artemis*, homeward bound with coal from Cardiff, went ashore under the gig *Gleaners* boathouse.

1868
The German Barque *Die Sonne* of Pillan bound from Cardiff to Barcelona with coal was wrecked at Praa Sands, her master Captain Bruno Burier had tried to run for Falmouth instead he became embayed and doomed in the West North West gale. She drove ashore on the Stones reef and then on to the beach at Praa Sands. Despite the attempts of the shore rocket crew who did get several lines aboard and before the lifeboat arrived from Penzance the *Die Sonne* was smashed to pieces. Captain Burier and his crew and two Scillonian pilots who had tried to get her into safety were drowned only yards from the safety of the shore.

The wreck of the Gypsy – St. Ives 19th February 1868
The *Gypsy* was first spotted by the pilots of St. Ives labouring in a west north west gale. It soon became clear that the ship, clearly hard pressed, most of her mainsail had blown to rags and her other canvas was reduced to a small jib and a standing foresail, was in difficulty. It soon became clear that the schooners intention was to make for the shelter of St. Ives harbour, furthermore, just outside the harbour a bar of sand had built up known as the Ridge it presented a fatal barrier for any ship that should hit it. Similarly if the ship were to attempt to anchor in a gale such as was blowing at the time it was equally hazardous. The bay at St. Ives has a soft sandy bottom and the anchors

of the day would either simply slip through the bottom, or if the anchor should hold, there was every chance, in such a gale, that the cables would part. In such a case the vessel would drive before the gale across the bay either on to the rocks of the Stones reef and Godrevy or on to Gwithian Beach.

On seeing the danger the youngest pilot was sent running into St. Ives to raise the alarm and get the lifeboat alerted. Whilst the lifeboat was being prepared the schooner the old *Gypsy* of Chepstow had rounded the island in mountainous seas. A huge crowd had assembled on the old (now destroyed) wooden pier which at that time formed a second harbour outside the granite Smeatons pier. Then it happened, the *Gypsy* struck the sandbar outside the harbour. In the lifeboat house the St. Ives boat *Moses* was in the process of being launched and many willing hands gathered and took the strain at the carriages towropes, however, with the tide out, the launch promised to be a long and difficult process. In view of this some of the local fishermen and pilots resolved to rescue the crew of the stranded *Gypsy* using their six oared gigs. Later it was said that the gigs crews were goaded into action by certain malcontents who had made accusations regarding the *Moses* crew failing to do their duty in the recent wreck of the French collier brig *Courvier du Nord* when despite gallant attempts to effect a rescue, six of the Frenchmans crew were drowned.

The gigs *Theodore, Express* and *Nimble* were launched with much difficulty but great encouragement from the outer harbour. At the same time the incoming tide had, with the effect of the pounding surf, wrenched the *Gypsy* clear, and with the aid of the few rags of sails drove her right in onto Porthminster Beach, where she just wallowed, at times completely shrouded in driving clouds of spray. The crew of the rocket apparatus racing toward her first stranding had to be diverted to her new wreck site.

The gigs labouring through the maelstrom were soon caught up by the *Moses* and as the four rescuers reached out toward the open sea they lost the shelter of the land. The seas already huge, took on mountainous proportions, then one wave, greater than those that had preceded it, rose like a sheer wall, the *Theodore* rose on its back up to the crest and the wave shook her from stem to stern, then passed on, leaving the gig unscathed, but building in power, strength and speed it next swept up to the *Express* and hurled her, crew and all, with terrific force straight onto the bows of the *Nimble* and capsized; all the *Express's* crew being tossed into the water; sweeping on, the wave next hit the *Moses* tearing three of her crew overboard.

The *Nimble's* crew on recovering their breath went to the assistance of the seven crew of the *Express*, all of whom were floundering in the water. With five crewmen recovered on board and one man clinging to the upturned *Express* the other crewman of the *Express* Nicholas Jacobs was seen a short distance off but before he could be recovered he sank beneath the waves and was drowned. As his outstretched arm disappeared beneath the waves a great cry went up from the women on the shore. Nicholas Jacobs was 37 years old, a father of six small children. Meanwhile the *Moses* had recovered her three men overboard, one of these, the coxswain Edward F. Toman, suffered severe injuries. Having got her own crew aboard Moses then rescued the last member of the gig *Express*. The gigs *Theodore* and *Nimble* by this time had struggled back to shore the boats full of water and the crews half dead. On reaching the shore the crews had to be carried ashore and several required support to reach their homes.

The rocket drill performed by the team proved to be totally ineffectual, the distance being too great the rocket falling short of the wreck. The lifeboat, alone now, pressed on to its task, the *Gipsy* now began to submit to the seas onslaught and was beginning to break up. After great effort the *Moses* reached its goal and time after time she returned after being driven off the wreck by the elements on each return she plucked a crew man from the stricken schooner, finally the crew of six having been rescued the *Moses* made for the safety of the beach. Finally the *Moses* landed and her crew, and the crew of the *Gypsy*, and all were greeted by loud cheers by those ashore. The old *Gypsy* by this time had broken her back and gone to pieces in the surf. Captain C. G. Grenfell, Hon. Secretary, of the St. Ives lifeboat stated "There can be no doubt that the death of Nicholas Jacobs is in someway due to the meddlesome and inconsiderate criticisms which were heard on a recent occasion, when the services of the lifeboat were unsuccessful. These same persons were today foremost in urging on the gigsmen in their brave, but too hazardous, rivalry with the lifeboat".

1868

In December of 1868 the barque *North Britain* fell onto a lee shore in a heavy gale within the Mounts Bay. Unable to extricate herself she eventually drove ashore. Her predicament was answered by the inhabitants of St. Michaels Mount who launched both a pilot gig and an 8 oared barge but on leaving the lee of the Mount they themselves were in danger and had to turn back. At the same time the Penzance lifeboat was being launched from Eastern Green. Finally after a desperately hard row the lifeboat *Richard Lewis* reached the stricken barque. However before she could take on board any survivors the lifeboat was picked up by a huge wave and capsized. Thomas Carbis the coxswain was almost drowned in this incident when he became trapped under the ship when he was finally hauled aboard the righted lifeboat he was assumed to be dead. The stroke oarsman a man called Hodge was also washed away and almost lost, when he was finally recovered the rescue was abandoned and the *Richard Lewis* was beached. Thomas Carbis recovered later ashore. On seeing all attempts of help fail, the Captain of the *North Britain* ordered all hands to take to the ships boats. However one boat capsized and the other took a tremendous pounding. The lifeboat, freshly crewed, was launched a second time and managed to save the remaining crewmen before the *North Britain* went to pieces.

1869

In dense fog the steamship *Tyne Queen* came ashore on Men- a-Vaur rock to the north of Tresco, off St. Helens. Within a short time she had swung between Men-a-Vaur and St. Helens, but was still not badly damaged as soundings showed she was not taking in too much water. Her main damage was however, disabling, both her rudder and propellor were out of commission. It was not long before the pilot gigs arrived and the *Tyne Queen's* master anxious to save his ship asked for help in the way of a steam tug to be summoned at all haste. The gigs crews explained that the nearest tug was based in Falmouth and that whilst it was calm now, that by the time a tug had been obtained and made the voyage from Falmouth it was odds on that the weather would change and the *Tyne Queen* would be no more!

In the dead calm the sailing cutters could offer no assistance but a plan was hatched to tow the *Tyne Queen* off using as many gigs as could be mustered. Eventually seven gigs with a crew strength of 84 men all put ropes to the steamers bow and in one gigantic effort began the Herculean task of rowing the ship clear of the rocks. Eventually the steamer was towed into St. Helens pool through the narrow Gap Rocks entrance where she settled safely on the Sandy beach. The crews all supplementing their meagre incomes with a sizeable salvage claim.

1869

On the 16th February 1869 the gig *Linnet* went to the aid of the Dutch schooner *Alida* of Veendam bound for Tarragona from Swansea which wrecked in a severe south westerly gale on White Island of St. Martins loaded with a cargo of patent fuel. The crew of the *Linnet* had only just got the crew off as the *Alida* sank without trace. In this same gale the fog warning bell was swept out of the 100' high Bishop Rock Light by a wave and smashed to pieces on the rocks below.

Awards to crew of the *Linnet* for the *Alida* rescue. Thomas Goddard

(Master) Certificate of Honourable mention and a silver medal T. Goddard, R. Ashford (Jnr), J. Ashford, N. Ashford, J. Odger, T. Woodcock and S. Woodcock, Certificates of Honourable Mention and £1 per man.

1869

The brigantine *Thomas* of Poole in difficulties off Padstow was soon being attended by a local gig. The gig however was also soon in difficulties and needed to be saved by the Padstow lifeboat Albert Edward II who also managed to save the six crew of the *Thomas*.

Also lost same day, same place was the *Alexandrine* under Captain Sanjou from Swansea bound for Nantes with a cargo of coal. The *Thomas* also had aboard a cargo of coal and both ships may have been sailing in company.

1870

On 27th January 1870 the ship *William Poolman* of Rotterdam went aground to the South of Samson on a reef known as Southward Well. The combined effort of pilot gigs, local boatmen and a steamer got the ship off and saved her cargo.

1871

The Cornish Telegraph 28th June 1871 reported the loss of the 600 ton iron barque *Il Primo* (or Primas or Premier) bound for Greenock from Havana with a cargo of sugar. When approaching the Scillies the ship ventured too near to the Seven Stones and struck the reef, and immediately began to take on water. The long boat was launched but soon floated off as it had not been made fast. The ship began to slip into deep water and the captain and crew managed to capsize the gig they were in as the ship went down. As she sunk a seaman leapt from the ship and began swimming. After three hours in the water clung to flotsam he found and scrambled aboard the first boat. Then the current took him and he caught a last glimpse of his five shipmates still clinging to the captains gig and the others on some wreckage. He in his longboat without oars or any means of propulsion was eventually swept between St. Martins and Nor Nour where he was seen and rescued by St. Martins pilots in one of their gigs. No other survivors were found.

N.B. A far more colourful account of this wreck is given by Alf Jenkins in "The Scillonian and his Boat" where he says the survivor of the *El Primos* a Vicenzo Defelise was rescued by a pilot gig that found him clinging to the figure head (Now in the Valhalla Museum,

Tresco) of the El Primos (Il Primo, Primas or Premier) which was a life size carving of a woman.

1870

A Welsh schooner ran into Shipman Head but slipped off again drowning all the crew who had climbed out on the jibboom, except the captain who was found by a pilot boat floating upside down with only his boots showing above the water. He had previously refused a pilot boat.

1871

Five gigs went to the assistance of a large French ship which had, in dense fog, come through the rocks to Porth Cressa and stranded. The gigs managed to take the ships anchors and warps out into deep water and on the high tide the ship managed to haul itself to safety. It was then brought round to St. Marys harbour for repair.

1871

The four masted barque *Minnehaha* of Londonderry was wrecked in fog on Penninis Head in 1871. She was bound for Dublin from Falmouth where she had called for orders. Ten successfully made it ashore at low tide after a nerve racking night on the forecastle, which was held by the rocks. About forty years later a steamer of the same name was also wrecked (but later refloated) on Scilly Rock off the western coast of Bryher.

The barque *Minnehaha* was 845 tons and was bound from Callao for Dublin with a cargo of guano. She had a pilot on board at the time who mistook the St. Agnes light for the Wolf and ordered the ship to be kept away thinking they were passing between Scilly and the Wolf but almost immediately land was seen to the leeward and before anything further could be done the *Minnehaha* had struck Jolly Rock Nr. Penninis. The rock tearing through the ship from the stem to the fore rigging. The watch below never stood a chance and were probably drowned in their berths. The crew who got off the wreck did so by using the jibboom as a makeshift bridge. The ten who died on the wreck included the Captain, the Pilot and eight crew men.

The Wreck of the Delaware – December 1871

Built in 1865 in Ramsey, Isle of Man, the Liverpool registered steamer *Delaware* was a relatively new ship. At a gross tonnage of 3,243 who was not a small ship for the time either. She was 380 feet in length, was powered by a 280 hp. engine and was also rigged for sailing.

On the 20th December the *Delaware* was only a day or so from her home port outward bound for Calcutta via the Suez Canal. In her holds she carried a varied and valuable mixed cargo which included cotton, silks, sheet lead, tin and stationery and was manned by a crew of forty four. Early on the 20th December the *Delaware* was labouring heavily and making little headway in a severe North Westerly gale. The pilots on Bryher had noticed her and were alarmed at her progress and position which was bringing her steadily closer to the dangerous rocks and reefs on the outer edge of the Islands. It soon became clear that the *Delaware* was in real trouble and would almost certainly drive on to the rocks anywhere between Maiden Bower and Steeple rock. If she hit the infamous Tearing Ledges her fate would be sealed.

The *Bryher* men hurried to South Hill to get a better view and to be better able to judge the situation. It seemed hopeless, the *Delaware's* engines had stopped, it was later said they had overheated and stopped. On board the Captain and crew were fighting desperately to save the ship . . . and themselves. A jib was hoisted in an effort to steer the ship out of her desperate position and through the gap between Mincarlo and the outer rocks. For a short while it held, then it simply blew out, the crew desperately struggled to rig the stay sail, but no sooner was it up than the gale had also torn it to shreds, had either held, the ship might have been managed into a more sheltered position or even beached on a shore where the crew would stand a better chance of survival.

By this time, early in the afternoon, the *Delaware* was dead in the water without power, without sails and lying helplessly broadside on to all the elements. As she dipped her side into the trough of a huge wave she seemed to be engulfed by the following wave, when she rose, her bridge, masts and superstructure were smashed flat. Down she went into the trough of the next wave and simply never rose again, she had gone, in seconds, 3,243 tons of ship, her cargo and a crew of 44 souls. Finally being driven ashore on Norrad Rocks. The shocked watchers on Bryher guessed that if anyone could have possibly survived this calamity they would have been carried on the flotsam and debris of wreckage toward White Island and then onto the shores of Scillies largest uninhabitated Island, that of Samson. Almost miraculously five men could soon be seen in the midst of the maelstrom. Two men were clinging to a piece of broken spar, two more were hanging on to the side of a smashed ships boat whilst the other was on a piece of wreckage.

The Bryher pilots at once decided to effect a rescue, having decided it was possible; they launched upon their rescue plan. They decided on the Peters built gig *Albion* for their mission. Albion was built in 1844 and usually worked with the cutters *Rapid* and *A.Z.* She was 30′

in length and measured 5'6" wide. She had also been built with an extra strake giving her an extra 4" of free board. To make the rescue bid it was decided that the only possible launch site would be Rushy Bay about ½ a mile from *Albions* shed.

To accomplish this the *Albions* oars were lashed across her thwarts so that the boat could be bodily lifted and carried by twelve men. Assuming that the *Albion* was built similarly to all the other Pilot gigs from the Peters yard and allowing for her extra size it has been estimated that *Albion* was approximately nine hundredweights. Which would have given each of the twelve men would have had a burden of about 100 lbs. to carry. On reaching Rushy Bay, men were chosen to make the rescue mission at the oars, and one man, Patrick Trevellack, was elected as coxain.

The oarsmen were:	William Woodcock	James Jenkins
	John Webber	Steven Woodcock
	William Jenkins	Sampson Jenkins
	John Jacob Jenkins	Richard Ellis
	Thomas Bickford.	

Richard Ellis was left on the North Hill of Samson to signal back to Bryher by waving (or swaysing) his jacket if help was required. If help was needed the plan was to launch a second gig. In this case the other gig was the *March* probably built in the 1850's by Peters. (The March was built to beat the *Albion* which she did, the *Albion* was subsequently beaten by the *Golden Eagle* who was built for exactly that purpose. The owners of *Golden Eagle* being the owners of *Albion*. The owners of *March* not to be outdone ordered *Czar* to beat the *Golden Eagle* and so on etc. etc. etc.)

Finally the *Albion* was launched, and in huge seas edged its way toward Sampson and sought the lee of the North Hill. On finding the sheltered lee of North Hill some of the gigs crew scrambled ashore and climbed to the hill top to see how the situation had developed. In the sea they could see the two men on the half boat nearing White Island. As it finally reached the island the first man was seen to leave the half boat and grab a crag of rock, as the surf surged back the man was left high and dry, he then hauled himself over the rocks and reached the grassy shore. The second man remained on the ships boats side till it and he were washed on to the rocks he too made the safety of the grassy shore.

Whilst the men on the spar came ashore on the point of the island which is covered at high tide. They were observed desperately clawing themselves onto the rocks, then another huge wave swept them off

Some of the men involved in the herioc rescue of the survivors of the Delaware

Sampson Jenkins

John Jenkins (senior)

John Jacob Jenkins (and son) J. J. Jenkins was the first man to reach the survivors

Patrick Trevillick Cox of the Albion

Thomas Bickford – one of the Albions crew

MacWhinnie the Delaware's mate who survived

and they were drowned. The man on the flotsam was seen washed ashore in a totally exhausted state, near where the first two had landed. However, he made no attempt to reach the safety of the high ground and was swept back into the surf and drowned. No other survivors were seen but from their vantage point the Bryher men decided to take the *Albion* further down to the East Par of Samson then to carry the gig across the 200 yard isthmus and launch her again from the West Par of Samson. A quick conference of the nine agreed that when they reached White Island the four bow men would leap ashore whilst the remaining five would keep her safely afloat in the shelter of the island. The second hike with the gig began, this time over slippery weed, sand, grass and scrub, right into the teeth of a lashing gale with each step fraught with the possible danger of a stumble and the consequent damage or destruction of the gig. After what seemed an age, the crew fatigued, tired and desperate but determined, prepared to relaunch for the run from Samson to White Island. With the knowledge born of doing the job a thousand times the most suitable point was chosen to launch and the optimum time between waves was judged and *Albion* was relaunched without mishap. Soon their planned beaching drill was put into action and as the four bow men jumped into the surf they pushed *Albion*, and the remaining five crewmen, back into the safety of the deep water. The youngest man in *Albion*s crew was the first to reach the survivors he was John Jacob Jenkins. The survivors were the mate, a man called MacWhinnie and the 3rd mate, a man called Jenkins. One was bare footed and had no jacket, the other had no trousers. Both had armed themselves with stones in the belief that the Scilly Islanders would live up to the wrecking and pillaging tales told of these parts and would in fact murder wrecked crews. However, once assured of their intent the two survivors soon realised how misinformed they had been. The gigs crew first shared what clothes they had with the men then after a check to make sure there were no other survivors had been missed they made their way back to the waiting gig.

By this time the tide had fallen, further exposing more rocks and channels, and in the process, more shelter. The boat party expertly brought *Albion* in and the four crew and two survivors boarded and with the aid of a following wind soon made the return trip to the West Par of Samson. Again beaching the gig was an operation well practiced and was undertaken speedily and with precision. Even though stamina was severely sapped and limbs were aching, once ashore the final reserves of energy were almost tapped to haul the *Albion* clear of the high water mark. While they were recovering from their exertions Richard Ellis had been busy on North Hill signalling with his jacket that the other boat *March* was required. Whilst *March* was being rowed from Bryher the rescue crew and survivors made the hike back to the East Par where the survivors were kept as warm as was possible by getting into a rick of ferns whilst the rescuers huddled together in its shelter. *March* too, had to be carried overland on Bryher to Rushy Bay, once she landed on Samson she was taken over by the survivors and the crew of *Albion* who then rowed back to Bryher. Leaving *March's* crew to carry *Albion* back across the isthmus to East Par. This completed they spent the rest of the night beach combing for the remnants of *Dalawares* cargo that was coming ashore as the wreck broke up, and for any more crewmen who may have survived – none did!!

Ashore on Bryher the two *Delaware* officers, MacWhinney and Jenkins, were taken to the nearest house on the island, a house called Southward, owned by one of the rescuers – John Jenkins. Here after hot drinks the two men took hot baths to remove the coating of oil and tar they had acquired whilst being wrecked. The following morning every available man on Bryher joined *March's* crew on Samson to salvage what they could of the *Delawares* cargo. The men involved in this rescue never received any formal acknowledgement or reward or awards for this rescue other than the recognition of their peers that they had accomplished a truly miraculous feat with skill, daring and resolve, and their greater reward must be that their rescue mission has entered the legend and folklore of not only Scilly but wherever tales of heroic rescues are told.

1872

After being held up at Penzance long after her scheduled departure time the paddle steamer *Earl of Arran* bound for St. Marys was well behind time. One of the passesngers, Stephen Woodcock, who was a crew member of a Scillonian pilot boat, but not a licenced pilot, approached the *Earl of Arran's* captain.

He informed Captain Deason that he knew of a passage through St. Martin's Neck which would save time by avoiding the long passage through Crow Sound. Captain Deason said he knew of no such passage but Woodcock managed not only to convince him of its existence but also offered to pilot the ship through it personally. Inevitably when only part way through the Neck of St. Martins Stephen Woodcock drove the *Earl of Arran* onto a rock which critically damaged the twelve year old ship.

Fortunately the passengers, crew and cargo were all saved but the ship, which had been run ashore on Nor-Nour was later to become a total loss.

Captain Deason was tried and found guilty of a grave error in entrusting his ship to a passenger of whom he had no knowledge regarding his competency as a pilot, his masters certificate was suspended for four months as a result.

1874

On the 16th April 1874 the steamship *Zelda* of Liverpool on her maiden voyage from her home port to Palermo with a general cargo and under the command of Captain Pierce struck the Maiden Bower in dense fog. The *Zelda* was attended by two Tresco gigs and the crew were saved. Much of the cargo was later salvaged by divers. Some of the money earned from salvage on this wreck went towards paying Nicholas Peters of St. Mawes for a new gig which was named *Zelda*. The S.S. *Zelda's* career must have been one of the shortest ever, she was 32 hours into her first and only voyage when she was discovered by local gigs impaled on the Maiden Bower.

1875

The gig *Hound* whilst returning from Tresco to St. Marys on 10th July 1875 was capsized in a sudden squall. Those on board the gig had either been playing or watching a cricket match on Tresco. Four of the team were drowned. Walter Legg, Walter Hicks, Saunderson Phillips and W. P. Hicks. Those who survived were pilots Thomas Vingo, John Henry Jenkins, Thomas Hicks and shopkeep Augustus Jackson.

The Wreck of the Schiller
1875

During the night of 7th May the Islanders of St. Agnes had heard the occasional explosive signal. However, at first no notice was taken as it was a common practice for the many transatlantic liners of the time to salute the sighting of land with a salvo of cannon fire. However the explosions carried on throughout the night (this may have been the report of the pistol fired by the Captain to restore order after the ship had struck the rocks). The weather was foul, along with a dense fog, there was a wind that was rising in strength by the hour and a very high sea was running. At dawn the St. Agnes pilot Obediah Hicks manned his gig and went in search of the source of the cannon fire. Obediah Hicks' gig was the *O & M* built by the local shipwright Tiddy and named after its famous owner and his wife, (Obediah and Mary Hicks). The *O & M*, in huge seas, rowed out across Smith Sound, on past Melledgan and Gorrigan rocks and on past the Western Rocks of Rosevear and Rosevean; whilst resting in the shelter of

Crebawethan, after having rowed along the length of the reef of the Western Rocks, one of the crew, through the murk and mists, noticed what he thought may have been a ship to the south west. As the mists momentarily cleared the whole crew of *O & M* saw to their horror, the masts and some sails of a large ship protruding from the water in the vicinity of the Ratarrier Ledges.

The *O & M's* crew heaved on their sweeps and pulled towards the remains of what had been the day before, the German transatlantic liner *Schiller* of the Adler line Hamburg. The *Schiller* had 384 persons on board and some general cargo, mails and 300,000 dollars in coin for Hamburg, when she left New York, but when approaching the Scillies she had run into dense fog and no one realised she had passed inside the Bishop Rock until she drove, at half speed onto the dreaded Retarrier reef. The force and speed of impact left the *Schiller* with collosal damage, she was left with her bows firmly impaled, and with many of her bottom plates damaged she rapidly settled into the water at her stern. The huge waves quickly destroyed most of the *Schillers* own lifeboats before any attempt could be made to launch them. In fact at daybreak only two of her boats had survived the night.

The *O & M* took the passage through the Neck of Crebawethan with waves sweeping through the gap and many of them coming aboard the gig. Soon cries for help could be heard coming from the *Schillers* crew and passengers. The seas were littered with the debris of wreckage which posed an additional danger to the gig and its crew. A large piece of wreckage smashed into, and destroyed the gigs rudder. At the same time a survivors cries were heard nearby and a man was seen clinging to some wreckage. As he was being hauled aboard, the crews attention was drawn to other survivors seen in the water, either swimming or clinging to wreckage. With her manoeverability extremely limited owing to the loss of her rudder and because of the danger of damaging her ¼" planking on the flotsam, the *O & M's* crew could only manage to save four of the six people seen. However another gig (which may have been another St. Agnes gig *Stephen*) had arrived and managed to save the other two men. By this time the fog had lifted a little and the wreck along with masses of people clinging pitifully to the rigging could clearly be seen. Their awful cries and screams could clearly be heard above the sound of the crashing surf. Obediah Hicks with five survivors aboard *O & M* quickly realised that to take on any more in the weather and sea conditions would be to imperil all aboard. He also knew that if he could make for St. Marys he could alert not only other boats, but if he could get back before 8 a.m., they could bring the new Hayle built, Scilly – Penzance mail steamer, *Lady of the Isles* to their rescue.

On the way to St. Mary's the *O & M* met two fishing boats riding out the storm. They were alerted to the presence and position of the wreck and did in fact go to the wreck and save another five men.

At 7 a.m. the *O & M* landed in St. Mary's and by 8 a.m. the Mail Steamer had steamed up and left for the *Schiller* taking in tow the St. Mary's lifeboat the *Henry Dundas* and the *O & M*. The huge seas soon had the decks of the *Lady of the Isles* completely awash and the *O & M* pounded so badly in the tow that she cut herself free after two of her bottom planks were stove in. The crew of the *O & M* only just made it back to Scilly, baling all the time in order to remain afloat. By the time the steamer and lifeboat had arrived, the masts of the *Schiller*, along with the survivors, had succumbed to the seas pounding and had fallen. The *Schillers* two surviving lifeboats had been success-fully launched previously in a brief lull and did in fact make it to safety by landing on Tresco. The *Lady of the Isles* and the *Henry Dundas* now surveyed a scene of horror and desolation, all they found was bodies and 23 bags of mails (originally destined for Australia and New Zealand). The *Schiller* had been one of the largest ships in the world, now she was a mangled heap of wave smashed wreckage. 335 lives were lost. Afterwards divers salvaged £50,000 in specie and 2,399, in 20$ pieces. Following the carnage of the *Schiller* the practice of liners firing a gun on sighting land was discontinued. In 1975 a German lifeboat came to Scilly for the centenary of the shipwreck of the liner *Schiller*.

1877

In 1877 the nameboard of a ship called *Voltri* was found washed ashore on Porthcressa beach. Gigs were launched and searched for the assumed wreck but the blue nameboard with *Voltri*, in gilt letters was all that was ever found.

1877

A Scillonian Customs cutter and gig were offered for sale at £50.

1878

The gig *Hope* (which it is considered was the last gig to undertake a trip to France for the purpose of smuggling) was launched from her house at Porthcressa to assist in saving the crew of the French ship *Minerve* ashore on Morning Point. The gig *Hope*, pilot Walter Bickford of the St. Marys pilot cutter *Presto* (No. 17) took charge. The gig battled through huge seas being driven by a full south westerly gale. In the process of saving one of *Minerve's* crew from the surf several of the gigs oars were broken. The rest of the crew were saved by the life saving rocket crew. For her part in the rescue the gig *Hope* was awarded the sum of £20 and £1.50 for broken oars.

1878

The ship *Integrity* with her mast smashed and in danger of driving down onto the Western Rocks in the full fetch of a north westerly storm was spotted by the St. Agnes pilots. Pilot Stephen Hicks mustered two crews and in a rescue similar to that undertaken on the *Delaware* seven years previously. Two gigs were carried overland and launched into the oncoming sea and weather, one crew rescued the *Integrity's* crew whilst the other crew boarded her and managed to run the ship ashore and secure her with her own cables. Several days later the pilots returned and using their gigs *O & M* and Stephen Hicks gig *Stephen* and the steam tug *Flambeam* they managed not only to refloat the *Integrity* but to tow her from Porth Coast to St. Mary's for this action they were awarded £195.

1878

November saw the St. Agnes pilot gigs again called out to rescue the crew of a boat wrecked on the uninhabited island of Annet.

1878

The pilots of St. Martins were the first to spot the schooner *Surprise* or what was left of her some miles to the North of Round Island. When they reached the *Surprise* the gig pilots found the ship dismasted and abandoned. After cutting the rigging and fallen masts and spars free they were joined by the Bryher pilot cutter *A. Z.* and the two crews agreed to join forces and share the prize. In the northerly wind the *Surprise* loaded with pit props was jury rigged with the gigs lug sails set on the remains of the *Surprises* masts and taken in tow by the *A. Z.* The *Surprise* was finally taken into New Grimsby without taking any further help from any other source.

1879

The gig *Czar* on her first day with her new owners on Bryher attended two wrecks, those of . . .

The barque *River Lune* sailing in ballast was wrecked on the Three Brothers at the back of St. Agnes, all of her crew was saved, her figurehead is in the Valhalla museum. Later that night the barquentine *Maipu* with a cargo of saltpetre for the gunpowder industry was wrecked when she ran ashore in Hell Bay at the back of Shipmans Head. Again all hands were saved and part of her stern board is also preserved at the Valhalla museum at Tresco.

1879

On the 6th January 1879 the 130 ton schooner *Forest Deer* which had been built only a short distance away at Quay in 1867 drove into Fly Cove, Newquay. Under the command of Thomas Solomon she had been on a voyage from Gloucester bound for Porthleven with a cargo of salt her crew was rescued by a Newquay gig but *Forest Deer* became a total wreck.

1880

11th March – The Italian 706 ton barque *Barnardo* foundered on or near the many rocks and shoals around the Island of Annet. The gig *O & M* was dragged across the island of St. Agnes by her crew and the help of two horses to effect a rescue. When a man was sighted on top of the rock known as Old Womans House. It transpired that this lone survivor was the captain of the ship, his crew had tried to put off in the ships boat when it became obvious they were going to become wrecked, they were never seen again!! The captain with a large wooden rosary around his neck remained with his ship. When his ship went to pieces the captain undressed and swam ashore, to Old Womans House. Amazingly his rosary was found on a beach on St. Agnes later and was returned to the captain. After the rescue he was taken to the House of pilot Obediah Hicks who clothed and fed him and then took him to St. Marys. The figurehead of the *Barnardo* is now in the Valhalla Museum, Tresco. To the amazement and one suspects the embarrassed amusement of those involved, it seems that the captain of the *Barnardos* greatest concern, was not for the loss of his ship and crew, all he seemed to request on landing was a hot bath and some face cream!!

1880

Saw the wrecking of an Irish schooner of 60 tons on the island of Tean. The crew was rescued by the St. Martins pilots in a gig and by the coastguards in their gig. (Each Coastguard station had either a gig or a similarly built boat called a galley. Peters of St. Mawes built many of them and also undertook repairs on them. The Klondyke now in the St. Mary's Museum was built for the Coastguard service in 1877 by the St. Mary's shipwright Gluyas).

1880

The St. Mary's gig *A & B* owned by the shipping agent Banfield was, during an exceptionally violent gale, washed out of her house on Porthcressa bank and swept 50 yards in land where she was dashed to bits on a workshop wall.

1880

October of this year saw the ship *Strathisla* apparently abandoned about 11 miles off the Bishop Rock, she was approached by the pilot cutter *Atlantic* A 50 foot pilot cutter built in 1868 by William Mumford and M. Gluyas of St. Marys). Only to find the St. Agnes pilots busily engaged in keeping her afloat. The St. Agnes men had beaten the cuttermen to the *Strathisla* by rowing out to the ship earlier in their gig *Slippen*.

Slippen was originally called *Bernice* when she was built by Peters of St. Mawes in 1830 for the pilots of St. Martins. She was sold to the St. Agnes pilots in 1869 and her name changed to *Slippen* but she may still have been known as *Bernice* in 1880. Another cutter the *Presto* soon joined them and a strategy for salvaging the ship was agreed. The St. Agnes men from *Slippen* (or *Bernice*) stayed aboard and either steered or manned the pumps whilst the two cutters *Atlantic* and *Presto* towed the ship to port. The salvage of the vessel paid the gigs crew £45 whilst £15 each went to the two cutters.

1881

On the night of the 17th and 18th January 1881 the French, 82 ton schooner, *Charlotte Dunbar* of Lorient carrying a cargo of coal from Newport to Audierne was wrecked on Burnt Island, Alf Jenkins maintains her crew was saved by St. Agnes pilots but the Isles of Scilly Museum Publication "Shipwrecks Around The Isles of Scilly" records no survivors of the crew of five.

1881

Alf Jenkins records that in this year the pilots of Tresco and Bryher received £84 for saving the German brigantine *Kron Prinz von Preussen* and a further payment of £75 for the rescue of the Italian barque *Celina*, and £300 for saving the Norwegian barque *Arracas*. I can find no other mention of these incidents, though I have no doubts as to the authenticity of Alf Jenkins account.

1881

November 27th 1881 – The German Barque *Excelsior* of Hamburg from Rangoon for Scilly for orders, its cargo of rice, teak and rattan cane, had run into St. Marys roads for discharging orders and was forced to remain to shelter from a strong North Westerly gale. Then both her anchor cables parted and from that moment onwards the *Excelsior* was in danger. The pilots of Bryher saw the drama unfold and had soon launched a gig from the east side of the Island. In the strong gusts of the squalls the gigs oars kept blowing out of the thole pins but with the weather oars double banked and the mizzen sail set they managed to reach the upper side of the Roads where they were almost capsized by a terrific squall, they would have hove to at this point but for one of the crew having spotted a rival gig with every oar double banked coming across the Roads and gaining on the ship with every stroke. The Bryher gig spurred on by this, heaved on their oars with extra vigour. Both gigs and the St. Marys lifeboat reached the barque at exactly the same time on opposite sides and their coxswains raced aft only to find the Captain dead drunk. The gig crews agreed to take control and share any salvage. The gigs were cast off with only a cox and two oarsmen in each with instructions to run the gigs downwind and beach them where they could. The men left aboard slipped the cables of the barque, hoisted the foresails and wore off and ran onto the bar at Crow Sound. The ship was now leaking badly so all plans of making for Falmouth were abandoned. Their only option was to make for Higher Town Bay at St. Martins and beach her. The St. Martins men launched their gig and came out to help. The ship was finally beached on Cruthers Point, St. Martins.

The St. Marys lifeboat that had joined the gigs and taken part in the task of saving the ship she stood by throughout the night and eventually returned to her station after sixteen hours on duty. During the following couple of months the *Excelsiors* cargo of Rangoon rice was gradually discharged, her damaged hull was temporarily patched and made ready for more extensive repairs at St. Marys.

On January 22nd the steamer *Queen of the Bay* was taken alongside to provide extra pumping power and the packet steamer *Lady of the Isles* was engaged to make the tow to St. Marys. However in recrossing Crow Bar the *Excelsior* touched the bottom which caused her to lurch on top of her escort, *Queen of the Bay* snapping her mast. In the process of extricating the *Queen of the Bay* the barque settled down onto her side and the water flooded into her holds. The next few moments were chaotic as the Islanders engaged to keep the ship pumped dry made their rapid escape. The *Excelsior* became a total loss becoming a navigational hazard which needed a wreck buoy to mark her position for many years to come.

1882

Pilot gigs at Padstow assisted the stranded French schooner *Maria* of Granville by bringing out hawsers from stepper Point but before the *Maria* could be hauled to safety she keeled over on the Doom Bar and sank.

1882

On December 5th the steamship *Rhymney* from Cardiff and bound for St. Nazaire, France was seen by Pilot Robert Ashford of St. Martins some distance off Crow Sound apparently sinking. He immediately went out to the ship in one of the gigs. By the time Pilot Ashford had got the ship into St. Marys Roads the bows of the *Rhymney* were already nearly underwater. The pilot decided to get her beached as soon as possible, but when passing between the ledges, Cow and Bacon, the ship was swept to port and struck Crow Rock. Fortunately three more gigs came out from St. Marys and using anchors and cables she was eventually winched to safety. Her cargo of coal was transferred to other vessels and the ship eventually was repaired and returned to service.

1883

On the 9th of February the Welsh brig *Criccieth Castle* of Carnarvon, a 218 ton ship under the command of Captain Morris, sailing from Fray Bentos (the port in Uraguay not the Corned Beef Manufacturers) to Liverpool via Falmouth with a cargo of patent guano, struck Peninnis Head in a gale of wind in the middle of the night. All six of the crew and a pilot from Falmouth were drowned. The *Criccieth Castle* was a total wreck, Porthcressa beach was littered with wreckage for weeks after the event.

1884

The race for the abandoned ship *Crystaline* registered in Liverpool was between two of St. Martins gigs initially, but before the saga unfolded it involved no less than four gigs and the governor of Scilly's steam launch. The Lower town gig, under pilot Robert Ashford, was first to leave St. Martins and first to send a pilot aboard the abandoned ship. Once aboard they found the ship balanced between sinking and staying afloat, her holds 1/2 full of water and her bows dipping beneath the waves. Acting with caution borne of experience, Robert Ashford called his men back aboard the gig and stood by. Shortly after the Higher town gig under the command of Douglas Skinner arrived. He quickly siezed the opportunity and gambling that *Crystaline* would stay afloat, claimed her. He soon realized however that if anyone was to benefit from this wreck they would have to work together. So it was that the Lower and Higher town gigs joined forces. Progress toward port was painfully slow, the water logged ship laboured on but made little speed. The light easterly wind was in the right direction but with her poop high in the air steerage was poor and maintaining a course very difficult. So the two gigs were brought

107

to the bow to help keep the ship in the right direction. Shortly after two more gigs arrived and were cut in on the salvage, they too joined the towing force. After many hours at the oars and with the harbour in sight the fickle wind dropped completely, the oarsmen resolutely stuck to their task. However, it must have been a great relief for everyone when after a further several hours had passed, with no noticeable progress having been made, that the governors steam launch arrived and lent its assistance.

1885

On December 17th of 1885 the Steamship *Sussex* owned by Messrs. Morrel and Williams of London, ran aground on the ledges near Maiden Bower. She was bound from Baltimore to London with a general cargo and 200 head of cattle. Almost as soon as the stranding occurred the vessel was attended by the gig *Golden Eagle* which proceeded to safely land a large number of the crew of 40. When day broke it became apparent that the *Sussex* was still largely together and stranded far enough out of the water for the crew to return and salvage their own belongings. The captain returned and secured the ships papers, the chronometer and other instruments. Wrecks such as this were very profitable for the gigs. The cattle were generally lashed by the horns to the sides of the gigs up to six at a time and swum ashore. Salvaging cattle could demand prices as high as £5 a head, even burial of the carcasses of those that died, paid. For burying carcasses off the *Sussex* the Islanders were paid £1 per head. There is an instance recorded in Juliet du Boulays "Wrecks of the Isles of Scilly" where a man who had received £1 for burying a bullock off the *Sussex* was later asked to give the money back, when the Receiver of Wreck found that he had towed the carcass to land in the first place!

The money raised by the Bryher pilots by salvage fees on some of this wreck was used to commission the building of the gig of the same name *Sussex* which was built by Peters in 1886, now owned by Ralph Bird, shipwright at Devoran and builder of many of the fine 32′ copies of Treffry over the past few years.

1885

December 30th, about 1.30.

Mr. John Jenkins, of Tresco, in company with Walter Hicks, of Tresco sailed out for wrecking from the *Sussex*. On return the wind came over the hills of Bryher, overturned the boat filled with bags of flour. Walter Hicks made for Yellow Ledge and J. Jenkins held on to upturned boat. Walter Hicks drowned. J. Jenkins rescued by a boat from Samson. Hicks' body was later found in the same place.

A Gibson photograph of the wreck of the steamship Castleford aground on Crebewethan where she struck on 9th June 1887, the gigs O+M and Gipsy managed to save a total of 450 cattle from this wreck. One gig can be seen rowing away from the ship. The sails of another can be seen alongside. The cattle were taken to the Island of Annet and were later trans-shipped

1886

Alf Jenkins records that a report reads *Nellie*, Denmark, Brigantine 316 tones 27th March 1886, seven crew saved and two bodies recovered by St. Agnes gig, above shore on Meligan Saved by Osbert Hicks, Edwin Jenkins, Joe Hicks, William Francis, Grenfell Lugg, Edgar Wingate and Jacob Deason.

Meligan should probably be Melledgan a large rock or small island to the South of Annet or to the S.W. x W. of St. Agnes. Another report from the pilot cutter Agnes on the same date reads.

"When cruising on pilotage in position 2 1/2 miles SW X W of St. Agnes lighthouse we observed a man waving a souwester from a portion of a wreck lying in the Brow of the Ponds. We answered the signal and stood in as close as possible with the cutter. We got away our boat with four hands viz Walter Legg, Abraham Hicks, Stephen Hicks and Humphrey, who succeeded with much difficulty, in getting the only two survivors on the wreck brough to the cutter, exhausted. We supplied clothes and refreshments and proceeded to St. Marys. The wreck was that of the *Nellie*.

Charlotte Dorrien Smith in her book Shipwrecks of the Isles of Scilly says that *Nellie* was wrecked in St. Warnas Cove, St. Agnes (finally) after striking Jacky's rock and Annet. She says that Edwin Jenkins found a picture of a girl on the wreck and showed it to the mate (who survived) the mate said it was a photo of his sweetheart, the Captains daughter, who he had planned to marry at the end of that voyage, she drowned along with her father at this wreck.

Nellie had been launched at St. Johns, New Brunswick in 1866 as the *Julia Lingley*. As the *Nellie*, the ship had been on a voyage from Bordeaux to Cardiff with a cargo of pitprops, and had been involved in a collision to the west of the Isles of Scilly before she drove onto Jackies Rock. Nothing is known of the fate of the ship that *Nellie* collided with. However, the *Nellie* on striking Jackies Rock appears to have broken into two pieces, part of which drifted onto Annet the other into St. Warnas' cove.

The seven survivors who reached Annet are said to have quenched their thirst by drinking the blood of puffins caught on the little Island.

Later two more survivors were rescued, having clung to ships wreckage for sixteen hours. The Captain of the *Nellie*, Captain M. L. Svendsen did not survive, nor according to Richard Larn in his account, did his chief officer.

1887

This wreck occurred in the year of Queen Victoria's Jubilee. In dense fog on the night of 9th June, 1887 the steamer *Castleford* of Liverpool drove ashore on Crebewethan one of the most dangerous of the Western Rocks on the North of the infamous reef. She was bound from Montreal for London with a mixed general cargo and 450 cattle. The *Castleford* although destined to become a total wreck did not become a wreck that resulted in a loss of human life. Some of the crew left in the ships own lifeboats and reached St. Agnes, from there, word was passed to St. Marys and at about midnight the lifeboat went to attend the wreck and spent a large part of the night ferrying survivors to safety. A total of 450 cattle were saved from this wreck by the gigs *O & M* and *Gipsy* both of which were damaged as a result. The *O & M* was almost destroyed when a bullock panicked on the deck of the ship and came over the side of the *Castleford* onto the gig knocking out one side of her bow in the process. The *Gipsys* damage, by comparison was quite slight. She was merely pierced by a bullocks horn, a temporary repair being made by a crewman who bunged the hole with one of his socks. The cattle were swum alongside the gigs to the Island of Annet, where they were kept supplied with fresh water until another carrier could be found and salvage money agreed etc. Whilst the cattle were on the island one of them, a large bull, took it upon himself to commandeer the water supply. Eventually it was decided that he would have to go, and some marksmen were landed by the gig *O & M* to shoot him. After the deed was done the carcass was butchered and the meat sold at a knock down price. Even that caused complaints, as the meat proved to be as tough as old boots.

1887
The barque *Baynard* 234 tons of La Hogue bound for Cadiz from Liverpool with a cargo of Cheshire salt hit the Stones reef off Godrevy on 12th March 1887. Leaking, she ran for Hayle but was wrecked on the bar after an argument between her master Captain Lebel and the St. Ives pilots.

1887
On the 12th January 1887 the pilots of St. Agnes rowed round to the adjoining island of Gugh and saved the crew of schooner *Bonna*.

1888
In April St. Agnes gigs rowed off to the schooner *Princess Louise* of Barrow loaded with slates which was flying distress signals. With a bad leak and a cargo of slates the *Princess Louise* was in a perilous state. On boarding the ship, the pilots found the crew exhausted having been at the ship's pumps for hours. Pilots Osbert Hicks and

W. A. Mortimer took over the pump and James Thomas Hicks took over the helm and brought the ship and crew into safety.

1888
Other wrecks in the Scillies in 1888 which became total shipwrecks were the *Galoise* of Bordeaux which was followed by the *Bernardo* and the *Gomes*.

1888
St. Martins pilots using a gig with a crew of eleven managed to kedge and winch the 141 ton brigantine *Maria Stella* off Brancy Point on St. Martins. As the tide rose the men at the ships winches hauled in on the kedge anchor and the bower anchor that had been carried out by the gigs crew. The ship was eventually sailed in to safety the pilots claiming a £100 for their services.

1890
On the 3rd May 1890 in thick fog and high winds and seas pilots saw a ship at anchor only yards from the Retarrier Reef, she was the *Antares of Nantes*, bound for Llanelly with pit props. Two gigs failed to reach *Antares* but the lifeboat managed to get four men and a pilot aboard who got the ship out of danger aided by the St. Marys lifeboat *Henry Dundas*.

1891
The 60 ton Padstow schooner *J. K. A.* foundered on the Shag Rocks near the Mouls on 11th November 1891. When nearing the Scillies the J. K. A. laden with 86 tons of oats encountered huge seas being whipped up by a moderate gale. Early on the morning of 11th November the *J. K. A.* was hurled onto her beam ends, when she righted herself it was found that her port bulwarks and all her loose fittings on deck had been washed away. Her boom then crashed over her starboard quarter smashing that sides bulwarks and rendering her steering geer useless. By 6.45 a.m. *J. K. A.* had drifted toward Great Innisvouls and the crew made a futile attempt to drop anchor, both of which parted their cables. Causing the *J. K. A.* to drive onto the rocks. The crew being forced to abandon ship, made their way to Great Innisvouls, whilst the *J. K. A.* drifted clear and became a total loss. The *J. K. A.'s* crew was later rescued by a gig from St. Martins.

1893
The *Serica* was a 1,736 ton, steel, screw steamship, built in Sunderland in 1888 and also rigged as a fore and aft schooner. She had left Cardiff

on 16th November, bound for Port Said with a cargo of coal. Between Cardiff and Scilly, the ships master Sydney William Smith had been washed overboard twice, on both occasions he had managed to get back aboard but was left unconscious after the second incident. 1st mate John Parker was in charge. The weather that this ship encountered must have been incredible, her logs show that on the run down from Cardiff, she lost the tarpaulins from her hatches several times. At 11 p.m. on 17th she shipped a wave which gutted the main cabin. Seas had smashed all of her lifeboats and carried them away along with her main cabin, part of the lower bridge and everything movable in the bridge aft. Then another smashed part of the upper bridge and all moveables of the starboard side. W. Hiscox the receiver of Wrecks at St. Marys said when he visited the ship on 20th November "Nothing whatever was left standing in the cabin, the bulk heads were smashed in and the very floors torn up. The only wonder being that the vessel kept afloat".

Kept afloat she was though and after a few days in the St. Marys Road on the 24th November the *Serica* sailed from St. Marys Road in a "fairly well found" condition with pilot Abraham James Jenkins at the helm. The weather was fine and clear and the tide was at its lowest point but she had hardly got underway when she struck a previously uncharted pinnacle of rock in St. Mary's sound and began to leak badly. She was run ashore near the Woolpack Beacon to prevent her foundering. The pilot, captain and crew abandoned ship immediately as it was feared her boilders would explode; they did not, but the ship sank gradually as the tide rose. Salvage operations were carried out as the weather permitted until they were finally suspended altogether following a series of gales during the last week of December and the 3rd January 17894.

A subsequent enquiry exonerated Pilot Abraham James Jenkins and the small rocky patch, lying in only four fathoms of water not the eight shown on the Admiralty Chart, is now shown on charts as Serica Rock.

The gig *Serica* which was built by Tom Chudleigh in 1867 for the men of St. Marys was named after the wreck and the rock, and was the first gig to be built this century. The figure head of *Serica* was salvaged by members of the Dorrien-Smith family in a longboat (often mistakenly called a gig) called *Normandy*. The figurehead is now in the Valhalla Museum.

1895

On 2nd January 1895 the New Brunswick barque *Antoinette* which had experienced a frightful battering in a gale in the Channel and was drifting dismasted and helpless. A gig from Padstow went to her assistance but needed assistance themselves when they got into trouble. The Padstow and Port Isaac lifeboats eventually brought off the *Antoinette's* crew but the barque, stranded on the Doom Bar, became a total wreck.

1895

Whilst on a shopping and provisioning trip to St. Marys the St. Agnes gig *Daring* responded to the news that there was a ship in St. Marys sound flying a pilots pennant. The ensuing race to get a pilot aboard was won by the *Darings* crew. The ship, a large four masted Italian barque called the *Emmaneule Accame* was bound for Swansea from Bremmerhaven. The St. Agnes pilot Edwin Jenkins dissuaded the ships captain from his original plan i.e. to anchor in St. Marys Road and weather out the storm. Instead Edwin Jenkins figured he would bear away and approach the Road via Broad Sound. He argued that the *Emmanuel Accame* was too big and cumbersome to be tacked up St. Marys Sound. As he sailed the barque away to the south, pilot Jenkins shouted to his comrades in *Daring* that his plan was "to go off a piece to the west then come into the Roads via Broad Sound". This was the last the *Darings* crew or any on Scilly were to see of Pilot Jenkins. The weather worsened and instead of rounding the Bishop into Broad Sound the Barque carried on out into the Atlantic before coming about and finally making a landfall on the Irish coast under jury rig having lost all four masts in atrocious weather conditions. Eventually the ship was towed to Dublin, Pilot Edwin Jenkins, however, had been soaked to the skin on the trip out in the gig *Daring* and the long hours in wet clothes exposed to the vilest of elements in the depth of winter hastened exposure which led in turn to pneumonia and then peritonitis, he died in the pilots berth whilst the ship was being towed up river to Dublin. He was buried at Mount Jerome, Dublin on 16th January 1895. He was 38 years old and left a mother aged 76 a wife and six children. A fund raised by public subscription was set up to ease the destitute situation of his family.

1896

A wreck uncannily similar to that of the *Crystalina* which occurred in September 1894 occurred or reoccurred on 15th December 1896. When *Sophie*, a 533 ton Norwegian barque from Fredrikstad, was found in a derelict state by Bryher pilot Mr. J. Pender, at 8.30 a.m., in clear weather, lying about four miles north of Shipman Head Bryher, Pender and nine men went out to her in a gig in what he describes as a fresh northerly wind and a heavy northerly sea. He and four other men managed to board her and found her abandoned. Her steering gear wrecked but repairable. In the meantime, gigs from Tresco and St. Martins had arrived. With small sails set on the bow and the gigs assisting, she was run before the wind with the aim of making New Grimsby Harbour. When they were 2 ½ miles from land the *Lady of the Isles* came alongside and offered assistance which was accepted and she towed *Sophie* to New Grimsby, where she was eventually beached. It was subsequently discovered that *Sophie* was originally bound from Swansea with a cargo of coal and had been abandoned in a sinking condition on 14th December. All the crew having been picked up by a steamer called *Glenmore* and taken to Gibraltar. The vessel and cargo was later sold to T. A. Dorrien Smith, Lord Proprietor of the Islands for £250, the *Sophie* herself was dismantled, her timbers being used as fencing for the Tresco Abbey farmland. When the *Sophie* was initially boarded by the pilot J. Pender he was greeted by a "small well fed dog". Through this dog the owners were able to maintain, in court, through ancient laws, their right to the ship, and win their case.

1897
A disabled schooner laden with cod fish presumably returning from the Newfoundland fisheries was sighted off Bryher. One of the lifeboats and a gig went off to her and found her nearly awash. The *Lyonesse* was summoned to help tow her in, but she sank in Broad Sound.

1897
A lighter was seen off the Islands on Christmas Day and the St. Agnes lifeboat and a gig went after her and towed her to New Grimsby. She was loaded with railway rails and had broken adrift from her tow in heavy weather whilst in tow for Le Havre. The gig crew were paid £50 salvage and the Falmouth tug which completed the tow to Le Havre £80.

1898
On the night of the 15th December 1898 in a dense fog the steamship *Brinkburn* of London sailing from Galveston to Havre with a cargo of 9,000 tons of cotton, struck the Maiden Bower and became a total wreck. Her crew of English officers and Lascar ratings all landed safely in the ships own boats. The gig *Golden Eagle* salvaged many bales of cotton from this wreck. Most of the cargo was eventually raised from the wreck by divers.

1899

The gigs *Golden Eagle* and *Czar* were used in rescuing two crews from two separate ships on the same night. On the night of October 22nd 1899 and in dense fog, the three masted full rigged ship *Eric Rickmers*, on her maiden voyage with a cargo of rice from Bangkok struck Scilly Rock at about 11 p.m. and sunk. Five hours later at 4 a.m. on the 23rd October not more than 60 yards from the spot where the *Eric Rickmers* had struck the French three masted barque *Parame* with a cargo of coconuts also wrecked. The ships had been sailing in company a few days previously. The gigs *Golden Eagle* and *Czar* from Bryher were used to rescue both crews.

1899

The Steamship *Olivia* of Portreath which had signalled for assistance when entering Hayle in storm force winds actually hit the pilot gig coming to her aid. Fortunately the pilots were able to get aboard, but in the confusion the *Olivia* stranded on a sandbank, then summoned a lifeboat. The Hayle lifeboat *E. F. Harrison* came out only to be told that she was not required. In turning for home the *E. F. Harrison* was caught by an incoming wave and pitched onto the beach, fortunately without casualty. The St. Ives lifeboat also got into difficulties when one of her crew was washed out of the lifeboat but again all were recovered without loss of life. The local rocket rescue crew was also used but even their accurate aim was rejected. The crew walked ashore at low tide. The shipowners Messrs. Bain & Sons, Portreath were so embarrassed by the debacle that they made cash awards to all concerned.

1901

On 20th June 1901 in a strong southerly wind the four masted barque *Falkland* sailing from San Francisco, U.S.A. to Falmouth with a cargo of wheat, bore down on the Bishop Rock. Her master having success-fully weathered the Bishop took some avoiding action to clear the ledges to the south. Whilst coming about, the ship lost her way in tacking and became "in irons" bows on to the wind. The ship then began to move astern and before any remedial action could be taken crashed into the Bishop Rock. Much to the consternation of the horrified keepers of the light who feared the lighthouse and they themselves were about to be carried away. In the event, the *Falkland's* yards scraped against the tower without damaging the structure, but the *Falkland* now filling fast and sinking rapidly, settled into the deep water off the Lighthouse. Whilst the keepers raised the alarm by firing distress signals, the crew of the barque had successfully launched one

A Gibson photograph of a gig, possibly Golden Eagle, attending the wreck of the steamship Brinkburn wrecked on Maiden Bower Rock, Isles of Scilly in 1898

lifeboat and the captain were working on getting the second boat launched when the *Falkland*, by now ½ a mile from the lighthouse suddenly sank taking the captain and all on board with her. The St. Marys and St. Agnes lifeboats arrived shortly after and made a search of the area but found no more survivors, The Captain, mate, steward and three crewmen were drowned. The Captains wife and child and 23 men got off in their own boats and were transferred to the Islands lifeboats. The following day the body of a man was seen floating face down in Hell Bay at the back of Bryher, the weather was foul and a high sea was running so the Bryher men decided not to go out to recover it. However the Tresco men in their gig *Zelda* thought otherwise and went out to retrieve the corpse. However, they found that it was not the simple operations they thought it may have been, the seas by this time were such that it was impossible to turn the gig around without facing the danger of capsize, so the gig had to "back water" or go astern all the way back. The body they recovered, was that of the mate of the *Falkland*.

There were recriminations, the Tresco men accusing the Bryher men of callousness etc. in leaving the body. The Bryher men answered their critics by questioning the sense of endangering the lives of seven live men just to recover the body of one dead one.

1903

The iron, three masted barque, *Queen Mab*, 1,027 tons and built by Russell and Co., Port Glasgow in 1887 had been seen off the Scillies flying a pilot jack on 20th September 1903 but the weather was so rough that no pilots had been able to launch a gig to get a pilot aboard. So the ship eventually attempted to make her own way into the Roads. The *Queen Mab* had a crew of nineteen and had also got the Captains wife and child aboard. She was bound from South America (one source says from Iquique, Chile, another from Punta Arenas, with a cargo of fustic logwood. Fustic is a New World wood (usually from the West Indies or South America) which was used to produce a yellow dye, it was also used in tanning. Her captain tried to weather the Spanish Ledges buoy but failed and struck on the West Top several times but somehow managed to get through and made the roads and dropped anchor. however the action of anchoring is supposed to have been responsible for creating the vibration that shook free a large lump of rock that had pierced the bottom plates and broken off. The *Queen Mab* began to take in water. Shortly after this, the gig *O & M* from St. Agnes was able to launch and get alongside to get a pilot aboard. From St. Marys the gig *Leo* and the lifeboat *Henry Dundas* arrived and finally the St. Agnes lifeboat *James and Caroline* with Abram James

Slippen in 1907 before setting out to search for and collect the bodies from the wreck of the Thomas W. Lawson on Annet. The crew from left to right: W. Trenary, Albert Hicks, Mr. Cummings (a visitor), Ben Hicks, Jack Hicks, Israel Hicks, R. G. Legg, A. Hicks and standing in the water Osbert Hicks. Jack Hicks (5th from left) was the last pilot to board a ship, for piloting duties, from a gig in 1938

The seven masted fore and aft schooner Thomas W. Lawson. A letter written by Captain Dow and kept in the Peabody Museum Salem, Massachusets, names the masts: Fore, main, mizzen, No. 4, No. 5, No. 6, and spanker

Jack Hicks and Freddy Cook Hicks, St. Agnes, Isles of Scilly

Hicks as coxswain. The *Queen Mabs* captain offered two guineas (£2,10) to each man who helped with the pumping and £5 if the effort was successful and the ship saved. Crew from the *Henry Dundas* went aboard and began to help pump the ship; they remained at their task for seven hours pumping continuously.

The *O & M* took the captains wife and child ashore and summoned assistance from the steamer R. M. S. *Lyonesse*. Meanwhile crews from both the *Leo* and the *James and Caroline* had joined the effort to keep the water levels down in *Queen Mabs* holds, but to no avail, the levels were still rising. Then *Lyonesse* arrived and the gig *O & M* passed the towing warp and the tow into St. Marys Quay began. Several times the tow line parted in the rough seas, each time the *O & M* managed to get a fresh line aboard *Queen Mab* until finally she was edged again St. Marys Quay and on the low tide repairs were made that enabled the *Queen Mab* to continue her voyage to Le Havre. A subsequent salvage court made the following awards.

Gig *Leo* £6.13 for each of her crew of 10

Gig *O & M* £75 including the cost of 4 broken oars

St. Agnes Lifeboat £75

St. Marys Lifeboat £7.13 for each man

R. M. S. *Lyonesse* £1,250

The *Leo* was probably the last six oared pilot gig to be built in Scilly expressly for the purpose of pilotage, it was built by Samuel Tiddy and his son who afterwards became Captain of the *Lyonesse*. The *Leo* which at the time of the wrecking of *Queen Mab* was valued at about £50 was always the subject of much good natured banter between Tiddy Snr and son. Samuel Tiddy always claimed the side was built by him was better than that completed by his son, because when on the tack favouring the side that he had built, it always sailed faster than that built by his offspring. It is probable that when the salvage of *Queen Mab* took place that it was Captain Tiddy who was in charge of the *Lyonesse* and was being assisted by the gig he helped build!!

1907

The 4th December 1907 saw the wrecking of the largest fore and aft schooner that was or ever has been constructed. She was the seven masted *Thomas W. Lawson* built in 1901, by the Fore River Ship and Engineering Co. of Quincy Massachusets, for the Coastwide Transportation Co. of Boston, U.S.A. The *Thomas W. Lawson* was 375' 6" long and about 5,000 tons in weight. She was carrying a cargo of 60,000 barrels of parafin in bulk valued at $200,000 which was half as much as the value of the ship. The *Thomas W. Lawsons* voyage across the Atlantic had been beset by atrocious weather ever since she departed from Philadelphia for London on the 20th November. During the trip she had her lifeboats and rafts all smashed and washed overboard, most of her canvas was carried away, and some of her hatches were smashed. On making his landfall, the *Lawsons* Captain (Captain Dow) mistook the Bishop Rock for another ship. The weather was thick and visibility poor and eventually the captain found himself in the impossible position of not having enough canvas to tack and not enough room to wear the ship off. So he decided his only alternative was to anchor. He was in Broad Sound inside the Bishop Rock between the Gunner and Nundeep Rocks. The *Lawsons* critical position was seen by the Bishops keepers who immediately signalled the shore, a high sea was increasing every minute driven by a wind that was of gale force and steadily building in velocity.

The St. Agnes lifeboat was launched at 4.00 p.m. the St. Marys crew were away at 4.30 p.m. By 5 p.m. in failing light the St. Agnes Boat, *Charles Deere* reached the *Lawson* and asked if assistance was required, Captain Dow replied "No" but the St. Agnes lifeboat stood by, made fast by a rope to the stern of the *Lawson*. Shortly after she was joined by *Henry Dundas IV* the St. Marys lifeboat. Eventually Captain Dow requested the services of a pilot and William Cook Hicks (apparently known to Islanders as Bill or Billy Cook). The Captain, the lifeboatmen and the pilot all agreed that nothing could be done and their best chances lay with an abatement of the storm.

The St. Marys lifeboat in manoevering to keep station somehow managed to get herself under the *Lawson's* counter stern and in the heavy swell had her mast snapped. It was decided to return the St. Marys boat to her station and she was also asked to relay a request to summon tugs from Falmouth to the *Lawson*. The St. Agnes lifeboat also had a problem, one of her crew W. F. Hicks, who had got into the lifeboat without any form of waterproofs and as a consequence was soaked to the skin and was now suffering from hypothermia and exposure, it was decided that W. F. Hicks needed to be returned to shore immediately or his life was in danger. A signal agreed with the pilot, was that if the situation became any worse then the pilot would summon asssistance by burning a flare.

A keen watch was kept on the *Lawson* from St. Agnes and up to 3.00 a.m. the *Lawson's* lights were seen burning brightly then a fierce squall hit the area and in the rain and spray the *Lawsons* lights were lost, they never showed again.

When daylight came the worst of fears were realised, only the smell of petroleum and some floating wreckage showed where the *Lawson* had been. The St. Agnes pilots immediately decided to launch the gig *Slippen* her crew was Israel Hicks, Osbert Hicks, Obediah Hicks,

122

George Mortimer, Fred Cook Hicks, Fred Hicks, Williams Trenary and Grenfell Legg. Osbert Hicks was unanimously chosen as cox-swain, they set out toward Annet where most wreckage had been seen, they eventually arrived at Annet at 8 a.m. but found only three bodies lashed to a raft, then they found a living survivor who showed faint signs of life he was called George Allen and was an Englishman from Battersea. He was rushed back to St. Agnes where he was found to be suffering from exposure and broken ribs. He later died from his injuries. In the afternoon the *Slippen* was relaunched again and headed for Hell Weathers Rocks where Israel Hicks spotted two more men. Eventually one of the men was able to catch a rope and he was hauled through the surf and into the *Slippen* he was Edward Rowe of Boston and was the engineer. He was able to inform the *Slippens* crew that the other man was the Captain George William Dow and that he was severely injured. After Rowe was safely ashore the *Slippen* returned again to try to save Captain Dow. After many attempts one of the crew Fred Cook Hicks, son of the pilot who had perished on the *Lawson*, took a rope and plunged into the boiling sea, eventually he not only got ashore but also managed to man-handle the Captain down to the waters edge and to support him whilst the two were hauled back to the *Slippen* by the rest of the crew. Eventually the *Slippens* tally was, she had found three live survivors one of whom (George Allen) later died; the other two (the Captain and the engineer both recovered from their ordeal) and three bodies. The Captain was later to say that the squall that extinguished the lights also broke both anchor chains and that the wrecking was so sudden as to have made the sending of any distress signals impossible. F. C. Hicks was awarded the R.N.L.I. silver medal and was given a gold watch by the U.S. government and also by the *Lawsons* owners whilst the rest of the Slippens crew received gold medals from the U.S. Government.

1907

Running out at right angles to the coast at Gwithian from the Godrevy light in St. Ives Bay is a reef of rocks called the Stones. To a sailing ship in the vicinity of the Stones a becalming and a strong tide and swell setting a ship on the reef was almost as dangerous as a gale. On the 17th January 1907 the St. Ives Dandy, *R. G. D.* (or Roarding Great Devil as she was known) homeward bound with coal, was becalmed. Her crew knowing these waters well and sensing the imminent danger put a boat out and rowed to St. Ives for help. A pilot gig was launched and the *R. G. D.* warped to safety. The *R. G. D.* rigged as a ketch was later sold to the Thomas family in St. Marys during the 1st World War. No dimensions were given but Alf Jenkins describes *R. G. D.* as

A Gibson photograph of a gig, probably the Dolly Varden alongside the wreck of the Plympton which struck the Lethegus Ledges in 1909. Whilst salvaging the wreck the crew of the Dolly Varden: Percy Woodcock, Trevillick Moyle, Reggie Trenear, Edwin Jenkins, Harry Smith and Woodward Tonkin, were lucky to escape with their lives when the Plympton suddenly slid off the rock and sunk. Charles Mumford, another crew member, was drowned, and a visitor to Scilly, out for a trip, narrowly escaped wih his life

a 75 ton ketch. She was used as a collier up until 1917 when she was sold to Howard Edward Radford by her last owner Clem Thomas.

1909

In dense fog at 8.00 a.m. the Steamship *Plympton* loaded with Indian Corn and bound from Rosario to Dublin after having been into Falmouth for orders struck the Lethegus Ledge. The pilot Osbert Hicks of St. Agnes and all the crew had left her fairly upright on the ledge, but later in the afternoon as the tide turned, the ship keeled over. Later a St. Marys gig the *Dolly Varden* came out, her crew comprising of Percy Woodcock, Trevillick Moyle, Reggie Trenear, Edwin Jenkins, Harry Smith, Woodward Tonkin and Charles Mumford. Whilst working the wreck the ship slid off the rock and whilst most of the men swam to safety, Charles Mumford was taken down with the wreck and drowned.

Richard Larn in "Cornish Shipwrecks the Isles of Scilly" says that whilst the crew of the *Dolly Varden* were stripping the wreck, one of her number, a visitor to Scilly named Ormrod, was inside the deckhouse when the steamer capsized and sank. He went down with the wreck but managed to escape through a porthole, and actually came to the surface still clutching his spoils, the saloon stewards dinner bell!!

It is said at the time, that as a result of the experience that Mr. Ormrods hair turned completely white.

1909

One of the last of the large fully rigged ships to wreck on the Scillies was the 1,765 ton *Leon Bureau*. In dense fog the French full rigger, carrying a full cargo of Australian wheat, struck the Crim rocks which tore a huge hole in her steel plating, near her bows, the *Leon Bureau* with her crew battling to keep the ship afloat, drifted off the rocks and into the mists. Near the Seven Stones the Captain desperately tried to summon assistance from two naval torpedo boats but to no avail.

Finally a sharp sighted Trinity House pilot at Newlyn spotted the ship and on seeing her plight, went in pursuit. The pilot gig finally caught up with the *Leon Bureau* off Mullion and by this time the battle with the rising water levels was critical, the ship having six feet of water in her holds. At 5.15 p.m. on the 18th June, 1909 the *Leon Bureau* was finally beached alongside the eastern extension pier at Falmouth thus completing what had been a very difficult and tragic voyage.

Four months previously, whilst rounding Cape Horn mountainous seas had swept away the ships, binnacle, wheel, bell, rudder and topgallant yard and the bosun had broken his leg. In April the ships boy had fallen to his death from the rigging. Hours before hitting the Crims an A. B. had fractured his ribs in a fall and even when alongside at Falmouth the mishaps continued when another deckhand had his foot crushed whilst catting the bower anchor.

1910

Fog, the greatest danger to shipping until the advent of radar and electronic navigation claimed another victim on 18 April 1910 when the steamship *Minnehaha* a transatlantic liner owned by the Atlantic Transport Company which had been set north of its plotted course by the Rennell Current and had narrowly missed running ashore on the Shipman Head only to succeed by coming out to sea on the wrong side of the Scilly Rock and striking the reef on the south east side. Although the 13,433 ton liner had apparently suffered only minor damage and the sea conditions were flat calm there was a very real danger that she would suddenly slide off the rock and fall on her beam ends. It was at 1.30 am on 18th April that the coastguard reported hearing a vessel firing distress guns west of Bryher men launched the gig *Sussex* and by the time the St Marys men arrived with the lifeboat the Brycher men had landed the 66 passengers and 4 stewardesses in their gigs. The crew and the cattlemen were still on board however, and the lifeboat was asked to stand by.

As dawn came the fog lifted and later two Falmouth tugs arrived, part of the crew later transferred to one of them. Salvage experts decided the ship could be saved if she was lightened. Salvage took about three weeks during which all but 10 of the 223 head of cattle were saved by swimming them to Samson, afterwards they were transhipped to Tilbury. To this date cattle have never been put back on Samson. The liner company was extremely generous to the salvors of Bryher who benefitted from much of the jettisonned cargo which included, harmoniums, cases of pencils, cases of Old Judge cigarettes, Panama hats, penholders, curtain rings and rods, tobacco and some motor cars one of which was taken in tow in its crate by a fisherman, unfortunately it dropped out of its packing case before it could be got ashore. Even a grand piano was reputedly floated ashore. The *Minnehaha* was refloated after three weeks, after a great deal of work by the Liverpool Salvage Company under the direction of Captain Young. For their saving of the 66 passengers and 4 stewardesses and taking them across to St Marys and for other salvage and support work at the wreck the Bryher men were granted the sum of £500. It is said that for months after, everyone on Scilly from 5-95 was smoking Old Judge cigarettes.

1910

The 102 ton schooner *Belle of the Plym* originally bound from her home port of Plymouth for Glasgow with a cargo of pipe clay, was lying crippled outside the breakers of the Doom Bar on the 3rd August 1910. She had been badly damaged in recent gales and had failed to enter Padstow on the ebbing tide. The pilots however managed to get her in at midnight. The *Belle of the Plym* launched 1860 ended her days as a coal hulk.

1911

The steam trawler *Roche Castle* is reported by Edgar J. March to have struck the rocks in dense fog at the back of St Marys in the summer of 1911, and to have immediately started to sound her hooters for assistance. The gigs *Czar*, *Golden Eagle* and *Sussex* all set off from Bryher bound for St Marys Sound and on the way met the local gig *Dolly Varden* returning from a search at the back of St Agnes. *Czar* was rowed out along the back of St Marys to no avail and returned to the Road and saw a light and went to investigate. It turned out to be the anchor light of the *Roche Castle* which had been brought in on the high tide by Dick Legg and the crew of the *Shah*.

As no salvage was likely for the Bryher men they pushed off and headed for home. *Golden Eagle* got underway first, followed by *Czar* and then *Sussex*. It seems that at the point of departure one of *Sussex's* bow men grabbed the transom of *Czar* and jokingly asked for a tow home. In the same good hearted way the coxswain of *Czar* replied that the only hope *Sussex's* crew had of returning to Bryher with *Czar* and *Golden Eagle* was by having a tow. The challenge offered, was accepted, and the *Sussex's* crew stripped off jackets and shirts and pitched in to a race. The calm mid summer night saw a great race as bit by bit the gallant crew of the *Sussex* hauled her first level with and then ahead of her rivals. Straining at their oars and running in sweat they managed to get the much beamier *Sussex* ahead of her sleeker rivals and keep her there, finally beaching her a clear 100 yards in front of the next boat.

1911

On 8th January the St Agnes gig *Elaine* was en route to relieve the keepers on the Bishop Rock (The *Elaine* was built by Thomas of St Ives for Israel Hicks, originally to relieve the keepers of Round Island. Israel then obtained the tender for the relief of the Bishop Light also). The gig was unusual in as much as it rowed only five oars. As the *Elaine* made its way out they saw through the mists, a ship which was sinking by the bow. The ship was the *Ardencraig*, a three masted full rigged ship, which, loaded with grain, had sailed from Melbourne and was making for Calais having called at Queenstown for orders. The crew of fifty three had abandoned ship and had taken to two boats. The gig *Elaine* took some of the crew aboard and the St Agnes Lifeboat took others from the second boat, there were no casualties. Aboard the gig *Elaine* at the time was the photographer Frank Mortimer who had come to photograph the lighthouse keeper exchange instead he received some 1st class photos of *Elaine* rescuing one boat and his cousin George Mortimer, cox of the St Agnes lifeboat, rescuing the second boat. After drifting for about three hours with her foreyards aback the *Ardencraig* was seen to sink in the North West passage.

The Marion G. Douglas
On the 27th November 1919 the sighting of an apparently abandoned schooner must have lifted the spirits of the Bryher Islanders after the hard years of the Great War. The Bryher pilots in the gigs *Czar* and *Sussex* went out to Hell Bay to investigate and found the American schooner *Marion G. Douglas* registered in La Havens. The *Marion G. Douglas* was found to be in excellent condition and fully laden with timber, she had, it transpired, sailed herself, unmanned all the way across the Atlantic, having been abandoned by her crew. The crew it seems had claimed that the ship had sunk and a fraudulent insurance claim had been made. Rather than falling foul of wind, weather or hostile shore *Marion G. Douglas* had, for her swindling crew and owners, embarrassingly, safely made the voyage unmanned on her own. The Bryher men lodged a salvage claim and were awarded £3,000 a vast sum in 1919. Almost every man on Bryher assisted in getting the ship into a safe anchorage and then on to Samson, Bryher, where she was finally anchored. It is said that she was moored with a fine length of rope which was used as a mooring from the ship to the Colvel Rock. Alf Jenkins was told by a Bryher man, when enquiries were made about the rope, that it "was eaten by shags"!! The *Marion G. Douglas* was later towed away to Glasgow by the tug *Flying Spray* on the 29th December.

1925
Following the attendance of the wreck of the French Trawler *Cite de Verdum* on the night of 22nd March 1925. The crew of the St Agnes pilot gig *Slippen* rescued twenty five of the trawlers crew, Jack Hicks, G. Mortimer, R. Legg, C. Trenary, G. Legg and J. Scott, the *Slippen* crew were all awarded medals by the R.N.L.I for their part in their rescue. The wreck of the *Cite de Verdun* occurred on the Rosevear Rock.

A photograph taken by a Mr. Mortimer who was aboard the gig Elaine to take photos of the transfer of keepers on the Bishop Rock when they came across the Ardencraig a 3 masted full rigged ship, homeward bound from Australia with a cargo of wheat, sinking by the bows. The Elaine and the St. Agnes lifeboat rescued the crew. The Ardencraig sank before a salvage operation could be undertaken in the North West Passage.

1927

The infamous Scilly Rock claimed another victim on the 27th October 1927. The steamship *Isabo* of Lussin – Piccolo Italy. The *Isabo* steamed on to Scilly Rock at full speed when she thought her position was 13 miles south of the Bishop. Another victim of the Rennell current?

The *Isabo* loaded with wheat and bound from Montreal to Hamburg, struck the North side of Scilly Rock in dense fog at 5 p.m. Fog once again proving to be the age old enemy of all ships nearing shore.

The moderate South west breeze soon developed into a gale which to cause considerable damage on the mainland over the next few days. The *Isabo's* situation was critical and the Captain began sounding distress signals. Ernie Jenkins on dirty weather watch on Bryher heard the hooter being sounded repeatedly and then the sound of steam escaping. He phoned the coxswain of the St Marys lifeboat and the lifeboat *Elsie* left her house at eight minutes past five. *Elsie* took a route between Samson and Bryher but because of the sense fog and rising seas it took several hours to find the *Isabo*. Meanwhile from Bryher the gig *Czar* and the motor launch *Sunbeam* with a punt, put out from New Grimsby. These three boats soon found masses of wreckage with survivors amongst it. *Czar* and *Ivy* pulled fifteen men out of the water and one man from the ship and transferred them to the motor launch *Ivy*. By the time the *Elsie* arrived the *Czar* reported that they had recovered sixteen men from the water but more were on the wreck which was beginning to break up.

By this time the sea was full of wheat which had emptied from the *Isabo* as she broke in half, *Czar* and *Ivy* made for Bryher, but the wheat was threatening to choke the cooling systems of the motor boats. *Ivys's* engine glowed red hot through lack of cooling water by the time she reached home and meanwhile *Sunbeam*. and half of her crew using the punt, continued to dash in and out of the floating debris to rescue survivors. A further eleven being got off, including the *Isabo's* master Captain A. Tarabocchia. By this time it was getting very dark and the combination of a high sea, a full gale and terrific amounts of flotsam and debris made all further attempts too dangerous to contemplate. All boats retired back to Bryher to either land survivors or in the lifeboats case to await a fresh mission at first light. A doctor W. E. Ivers came over from St Marys in order to sail with the *Elsie* when she returned.

When they returned they could still hear cries for help but heavy seas were now raking the wreck and to get near enough would have endangered the lifeboat and her crew. The coxswain approached the lee side of wreck and fired a line over the wreck, after the third attempt, a member of crew on *Isabo* rushed to retrieve the line but was washed overboard and was amazingly and skillfully plucked from the water by the lifeboat. Two more crew men were rescued in a similar fashion afrer being washed off the ship after sliding down out of the rigging, the fourth man left on the mast was dead, presumably from shock and exposure. Then shouts were heard from a rock, it transpired that they were from another survivor who was naked apart from his lifejacket, he fell into the sea whilst attempting to catch the rocket line but managed to swim to the *Elsie* and get himself hauled aboard. No more survivors were found. Altogether the number saved was thirty one with six being lost. Three of whom were probably drowned in the stokehold when the ship struck. If awards are a measure of heroism, then the rescue from the *Isabo* must be near the top of the league. In addition to two Lifeboat Institution Silver Medals and six Bronze medals and several vellums, the Italian Government awarded thirty eight Silver and Bronze medals. It is said that of the nineteen men on Bryher at the time, eighteen of them attended the wrecking of the *Isabo*.

1955

On the 21st January 1955 the steamship *Mando* registered in Panama 7,176 tons gross weight and sailing from Hampton Road for Rotterdam with coal, struck on Golden Ball Bar at 8.30 pm in dense fog. Because it was low water the lifeboat *Cunard* had to take a hazardous route between the Norrad Rocks and past Shipman head. As she was leaving the *Mando* with the twenty five crew members on board and two ships boats in tow, the Bryher gig *Sussex* came up and was also taken in tow. However after the tow rope repeatedly broke it was decided the *Sussex* should take in tow the ships boat containing the crews belongings. This was the last time a gig was engaged in rescue work. By a strange stroke of coincidence (or bad luck) the Italian cook of the *Mando* had been shipwrecked on Scilly previously when he was pantry boy on the *Isabo*, lost on Scilly Rock in 1927! At the time of this wrecking the Sussex was 69 years . . . young and had not been used for about 26 years, her previous outing had been in 1929 when she had been used to ferry Bertha Jenkins and her wedding party over to her marriage with Norman Darling on Tresco. Vernon Hicks one of the crew in the *Sussex* on the night of the wreck of the *Mando*, said a gig was chosen because of their shallow draught and the fact that they had no propellor to become fouled in the sea weed, or strike the bottom in the shallows, or amongst the rocks. Vernon Hicks commented that the *Sussex* "was as tight as a drum" despite her twenty odd years out of the water and "did not make as much as a cupful of water".

Newquay's Good Intent

AN A-Z OF THE GIGS OF CORNWALL AND THE ISLES OF SCILLY PAST AND PRESENT

This is by no means, a definitive or complete list, no doubt readers will be able to add to it. The author would welcome details to update this list in the future.

A & B
Where and when or by who this gig was built if unknown. *A & B* was a St. Marys gig housed on Porthcressa Bank owned by the Banfield's. Alf Jenkins records her as being smashed to pieces against Alfred Trenears workshop wall after being swept 50 yards inland during a particularly violent gale.

ALBION
A Peters built gig built in 1844 for the pilots of Bryher, she was 30′ 0″ in length by 5′ 6″ beam and was built with an extra strake to give her more free board.

Her most famous launch was to the steamship *Delaware* in 1871 see 1871 Wreck and Rescue Chapter.

Albion worked with the cutters Rapid and A. Z. She ended up being sold to Mr. Frankie Watts who cut her in half and converted one end into a large punt and the other into a sailing dinghy.

ARROW
An old gig from Padstow mentioned by R. H. C. Gillis in the "Pilot Gigs of Cornwall and the Isles of Scilly". Built and used by the brothers Richard and John Tredwen. (See Wreck and Rescue 1859 "African" off Padstow's Doom Bar.

ALARM

The famous Saltash oarswoman Ann Glanville first came to notice being accorded special praise in 1835 after her first rowing "win" in this gig – she was then aged 39 years.

ALMA

A Saltash gig from the 1850's.

ANNIE

Fowey gig mentioned 1877 Fowey Regatta £5 1st prize.

ACTIVE

Newquay gig built 1974 launched by Lois Gillis. Orange Topside, white bottom ACTIVE in white bow flag. 32′ 0″ x 4′ 10″.

Built by Tom Chudleigh in the old Methodist Chapel, Garrison Lane, St. Marys. Tom Chudleigh was assisted for a time by Harold Kimber a master boat building who on his retirement lived aboard a Maurice Griffiths designed yacht called *Brue Gull* which he had built himself. *Brue Gull* is still with us at Mylor though sadly Harold (Kim) Kimber is not. Kim was responsible along with and through a lengthy postal correspondance with an American boat builder John Gardner in drawing up the lines of *Treffry* now reprinted in "MORE BUILDING CLASSIC SMALL CRAFT" by John Gardner.

Active was built alongside another gig destined for Newquay the *Good Intent* both were copies of the Newquay gig *Treffry*.

Active, *Unity*, *Good Intent* and *Fly* all named after Newquay Pilchard Seine Company's and Cellars of same names.

ANN GLANVILLE

Built by Ralph Bird in 1990, launched by the Mayor of Saltash and owned by East Caradon Gig Club. Colour: White Topside: Red bottom: Black rubbing strake. A slim line copy of the *Treffry* 32′ 0″ x 4′ 9″.

Named after the famous Saltash oarswoman Ann Glanville 1796–1880. Ann Glanville nee Wherrin was a waterwoman who worked from Saltash between 1815 and 1850 rowing goods and passengers about the Tamar and its creeks. As a spin off from their normal days work the water folk earned pin money racing in regattas locally and in Ann's case, further afield, including a now famous encounter in Le Havre.

ARK

Name of a St. Ives pilot boat probably a six oared gig. Cyril Noall's booklet "The Story of St. Ives" records the folklore tale of "Jack Harry's lights it is said always appeared before a storm and the lights wre usually on the spectre of a ship that would perish ere the storm abated. One pilot has recounted the tale of how he and a crew in *Ark* had responded to a vessel in the offing. The vessel was, it appeared, standing off St. Ives head signalling for a pilot. The pilots in a strong West North Westerly wind put out of her and thought they had come alongside when the ship, it seems, "slipped to windward a league or so". The *Arks* crew went in pursuit and again prepared to board. The ship again disappeared only to be resighted in the vicinity of Godrevy. The pilots then realised they had been chasing Jack Harry's lights and aborted their mission and returned to port.

BEE

Built by Peters of St. Mawes 1838 for Pilots of St. Mary's, Bee was stationed at Pendreathen. Launched to the rescues of *Victoria of Exeter* as a brand-new gig 1838, later sold to St. Agnes launched to wreck of *Thames* 1841 (see Wreck & Rescue).

BERNICE or SLIPPEN

Built by Peters of St. Mawes 1830 for St. Martins pilots and worked from St. Martins until 1869 when she was sold to St. Agnes pilots and her name changed to *Slippen* length 28' 0" x 5' 4". Famous for her rescue of survivors of the 7 masted schooner *Thomas W. Lawson*. In 1907 and in 1925 she saved 26 lives from the French Trawler *Cite de Verdun*. Sold to Newquay Rowing Club in 1950's she was completely renovated. In 1975 she returned to Scilly. In 1980 she was sold to Scilly. She is still in regular use. Orange topsides, white top plank, white bottom.

BESSIE & BOY PHILLIP

St. Ives gigs mentioned in some accounts of *Cintra* gale 17th November, 1893 apparently the St. Ives lifeboat went to their rescue when they got into difficulties on the day of the infamous *Cintra* gale.

BONNET

Built the same year as *Slippen* (1830) for the pilots of St. Martins built by Peters at St. Mawes. Originally built 30' 4" x 5' 0½" beam but was "pulled home" by Obediah Hicks and narrowed by 2¾" to her present dimensions of 30' 4" x 4' ¾". By winning races in 1908/10, she won a trophy outright.

The *Bonnet* always had a good record as a sailing gig. *Bonnets* claim to fame (apart from her longevity) is that one of her early owners John Nance a St. Martins pilot in the early 1800's probably used *Bonnet* on most, if not all occasions for his 25 smuggling trips to France.

Her name reputedly came from the "good luck" imparted on her missions by an old lady who is supposed to have waved her magic powers to the boat and crew by waiving her bonnet at them when the boat was launched. She was bought by Newquay Rowing Club in 1953 and was extensively repaired and renovated by Mr. S. Brabyn of Padstow in both 1953 and 1956. In 1973 she was sold back to Scilly. In 1977–78 Ralph Bird undertook a complete refit on *Bonnet*. *Bonnet* is still in use. Colours Mid Green topsides, White strake and White bottom. Owned by the Gig Committee Isles of Scilly.

R. H. C. Gillis recalled talking to Patrick Ryan of Hayle in 1953 when Mr. Ryan was 88 years old. Patrick Ryan was the last surviving member of the 6 shareholders who brought *Bonnet* to Tresco in 1903 from St. Martins. He told Gillis that he could remember the *Bonnet* at St. Martins when he was only 8 years old. He also said that he left Tresco in 1920 and just previous to this *Bonnet* had been sold to Bryher, but evidently she had subsequently been repurchased back to Tresco, because it was from Tresco that she was purchased by Newquay Rowing Club in 1953. She was reputedly named after a witch on St. Martins known as "the old lady with the bonnet" who was supposed to wave her headgear in the general direction of boat and crew in order to imbue them with extra speed, strength and luck. Or was she originally signalling with her hat as the huers of old did to the pilchard sein boats; after all one of her owners was John Nance a known and infamous smuggler who may well have been glad of a semaphored message of the whereabouts of the preventive men?

BRANCH
An old St. Ives gig which survived until the 1920's when it was blown off the quay wall in a gale and totally smashed.

BLUEBELL
A Saltash gig which competed for the Queens plate and £100 at a race in Devonport in 1847.

BLUCHER
An early Scillonian gig which is on record with two other gigs *Dove* and *Champion* in assisting at the wreck of the Dutch barque *Borodino* in 1830 (see Wreck & Rescue)

BOOT
A St. Marys gig stationed at Pendreathen may have worked with the Pilot cutter *Bull* a 52' 0'' cutter first licenced by Trinity House in 1813 (when she came out worst in an encounter with a French privateer lugger). Her last owner Sam Guy used her as the family leisure boat, she eventually was left to rot and was used as firewood.

BLACK DIAMOND
An Old Falmouth gig owned by Bragdons.

BOLO
Old Hayle gig (name only, no other details)

BRIDE
Old Hayle gig (name only, no other details)

BLACKBALL
An old Falmouth gig owned by Fox's

BRITON
On old St. Agnes gig she assisted, with the gigs *Bee* and *Thomas* in the rescue attempt to save the crew and passengers of the *Thames* in 1841 (see Wreck & Rescue)

BULL
Peters built at St. Mawes in 1838 owned and worked by and on occasions, with the pilot cutter of the same name. She was also a new gig when with gigs *Bee* and *Juno* she assisted in the rescue of the *Victoria of Exeters* crew in 1838 (see Wreck & Rescue)

Bull met a tragic end having left her home port of St. Mary's to embark on some "free trading" in France she was last seen running before a southerly gale up Smith Sound. Her mizzen sail being used on her main mast, she was clearly in distress. The only remains of this gig or her crew was a piece of new wood that had only been fitted the day previously.

BULLER
This gig was built by the Devoran Shipwright, Ralph Bird in 1986 for the Cadgwith gig club. She is a copy of the famous Peters built gig *Treffry*. She is named after a local character from Cadgwith Mr. Richard Redvers Arthur known locally to one and all as *Buller*. In 1989 the *Buller* was taken to the Henley Royal Regatta. Dimensions

32' 0" x 4' 10". Colours: Light Blue topside, White bottom, Dark Blue top strake, Red rubbing strake.

BOSCASTLE
is known to have had a gig but its name has not been recorded.

CHALLENGER
An old Scillonian gig. Recorded by her coxswain being a signatory to a letter written in 1829 to the Customs which asked for a repeal of the law which forbade any more than four crew members being allowed in a gig. This desperate rule was made in attempt to stop gigs engaging on smuggling trips to France and also because a gig, if apprehended by a Customs revenue cutter, merely had to pull to windward to evade arrest. In 1829 *Challengers* cox was John Smith.

CIRCLE
A Truro gig mentioned by R. H. C. Gillis in the Pilot Gigs of Cornwall and the Isles of Scilly. There is a model of a gig called *Circe* in the County museum, Truro built by Ralph Bird.

In the 1950's a set of old moulds for building a gig were discovered in the Peter's sheds at Polvarth, on these an old shipwright had inscribed *PILOT GRIG – ARROW AND SURSEY* he knew what *Circe* sounded like but could not spell it.

CHAMPION
This gig was in the company of the gigs *Dove* and *Blucher* at the rescue of the barque *Borodino* 7th February 1830. On the 4th February 1836. She worked with the pilot cutter *Cyclops*. (Thomas Mortimer, master) in the rescue of the crew of *Fame* (see Wreck & Rescue). In 1829 *Champion*'s master is recorded as being Francis Hicks.

CAMPERNELL
Built by Peters of Polvarth, St. Mawes in 1895 as a gig for carrying – anything from flowers, to salvage, to coffins. Campernell is a very beamy gig at 6' 8" and her beam tends to make her look longer than her 30' 0" length. Built for the pilots of St. Agnes she is still on the island. Under the supervision of Ralph Bird, the *Campernell* has undergone an extensive renovation completed 1993 by students at the Falmouth College boatbuilding course and will be in good heart to celebrate her centenary in 1995. Owned by shareholders on St. Agnes, she is painted white with a blue topstrake.

CONSTANCE

An old Padstow gig mentioned in a Report in the Royal Cornwall Gazette in 1861 at a Regatta race in Newquay – £11 in prizes paid out at Newquay. 1st Treffry, 2nd Dove, 3rd Constance, 4th Zoe. *Constance* was kept at the Dennis yard and was painted Black.

CHIP OFF THE OLD BLOCK

The name of the last gig that the celebrated oarswoman Ann Glanville was in the crew of, in competition. This was in 1847 when Ann Glanville was 51 years old.

CLUMBUNGY

A Scillonian gig, mentioned along with the gig *Jolly* as being stopped from putting to sea by H.M. Customs in 1828 for smuggling offences.

CZAR

One of Scillies most famous gigs she was built in 1879 by Peters of St. Mawes, and is still very much with us. Originally built to beat the *Golden Eagle* a task she very rarely accomplished, the *Czar* made money for her owners on the day she arrived at Bryher. She had been towed to Bryher using the squire of St. Mawes yacht, *Sea Snake*. On the day of her delivery two ships were wrecked. First, the Barque *River Lune*, then later that night the barquentine *Maipu*. (see Wreck & Rescue) *Czar* made enough money from salvage on these wrecks to pay for herself on her first day. *Czar* is the largest of the original Scilly gigs at 31' 6" x 5' 1½". When she was ordered her pilots said they wanted a gig that could beat *Eagle* to which Peters replied "the only way to beat the *Golden Eagle* would be to have 7 oars", the pilots reply was "so be it", so the *Czar* became known as "the cut throat gig". Her greatest rescue was in 1927 when she, along with the St. Marys and St. Agnes lifeboats and the launches *Ivy* and *Sunbeam* attended the wreck of the steamship *Isabo* (see Wreck & Rescue). It is said that the *Czar* attended most of the wrecks that occurred in the Islands from 1879 onwards. In 1899 she was again on the scene of another double wrecking. Those of the full rigged ship *Eric Rickmers* which had run aground and wrecked in dense fog on Scilly Rock at about 11 p.m. on 22nd October and about five hours later at 4 a.m. on 23rd October they went off again after hearing distress signals to find the three masted Barque *Parame* wrecked 60 yards away from the *Eric Rickmers*, same rock, same night, (see Wreck & Rescue). On 27th November 1919 *Czar* and the gig *Sussex* found, laid claim to and salvaged the abandoned American schooner *Marion G. Douglas*. *Czar* had her keel replaced in 1966 and in 1987 appeared in the film "Why the Whales came" which was filmed on Bryher. *Czar* which has an impressive list of racing successes to her credit, is still used regularly and is still owned by the descendants of the pilots who had her built in 1879. Colour: red topsides – white bottom, yellow top strake, black rubbing strake.

CAESAR
A St. Ives gig mentioned in the diary of Captain Tregarthen Circa 1830.

"The pilot boat Caesar brought into the roads a ketch laden with fruit from Messina bound for St. Petersburg".

and

"The French Brig *General Foix* of Havre de Grace brought in by the Caesar. Four men washed overboard by heavy seas . . . all sails carried away. Vessel, the most valuable prize ever, brought in sugar coffee, rum"

CUCKOO
An old Scillonian gig now lost without trace. This gig was owned by a Mr. Buxton who ran a pilotage and chandlery business from his store which was later converted into the Mermaid Inn.

CETAWAYO
Built by Peters but date not recorded but probably around 1870–1880 named after the famous Zulu chief (Cetewayo did in fact land in Plymouth in August 1882 and was received by Queen Victoria). Originally built for the St. Ives pilots she was later purchased by the pilots of St. Agnes and was kept at Porth Askin. She worked with the pilot cutter *Agnes* which was the last cutter to work pilots out of Scilly. *Agnes* was built in 1841 and was working up to the turn of the century, she was finally broken up in 1902.

She was probably the fastest gig in the Islands, many regattas banned her from taking place.

In her last and finest race, which she won, she had been dragged from the bushes that had been destined to become her final resting place, and was hastily bodged into shape for her final swansong, when the men of St. Agnes noticed that the usual Race Notice "Cetewayo banned" had been omitted.

The *Cetewayo* patched with brown paper, rags and tar, her gaping seams filled with soft soap, (which hardens in salt water), stayed together until the race was over and she had won, then she simply disintegrated on the beach. Gullis gave the date of this race as 1903, others the date as 1904. A photo, included in the book, from Frank

Newquay's gig Active built by Tom Chudleigh in 1974

Caradon's gig Ann Glanville (with a Hayle crew) built by Ralph Bird 1990

Cadgwith gig club's Buller built by Ralph Bird 1976

The Peter's built gig Bonnet built 1830, 30'4'' x 4'9''

Port Isaac's gig Corsair built by Peter Revely 1991
(photo: Jack Buzza)

Czar built by Nicholas Peters 1879
(photo: Jack Buzza)

*Cape Cornwall Gig Club's Cape Cornwall – Roseland Gig Club's Rhos
Cadgwith Gig Club's Socoa*

*Padstow Gig Club's Dasher built by Peter 'Dasher' Reveley in 1989
(photo: Chris Barrett)*

St. Martin's gig Dolphin, built by Tom Chudleigh 1969
(photo: Jack Buzza)

Porthleven's gig Energetic built by Ralph Bird 1991
(photo: Jack Buzza)

147

Energy built by students of Falmouth Technical College under Ralph Birds supervision, 1983–5

Devoran Gig Club's Fear Not built by Ralph Bird in 1991

Falmouth gig Fury, built by Ralph Bird 1992

Mevagissey Gig Clubs Endeavour, built by Foord & Dudley, 1988

Newquay's gig Fly, built by Ralph Bird 1993

Newquay's Good Intent, built by Tom Chudleigh, 1975

St. Mary's gig Golden Eagle, built by Nicholas Peters in 1870

River Yealm Pilot gig Hornet formerly owned by Newquay Gig Club and named Unity, built by Tom Chudleigh in 1978

Isles of Scilly gig Islander built to compete with the new 32'0'' gigs from the mainland by Tom Chudleigh in 1989

Isis, built by Ralph Bird, 1993 at her launch at Hayle

*Mounts Bay Gig Club's Lyonnesse, built by Ralph Bird, 1988
(photo: Mike Williams)*

Charlestown Gig Club's Mystery, built by P. Foord in 1991

153

Men 'a' Vaur, built for Tresco and Bryher in 1983 by Gerald Pearn

St. Mary's gig Nornour, built by Gerald Pearn in 1971
(photo: Jack Buzza)

St. Ives Gig Club's Porthminster, built by P. Foord in 1992

Roseland Gig Club's William Peters, built by Ralph Bird in 1987

*Rhos, built for Roseland Gig Club in 1989 by Ralph Bird
(photo: Michael Williams)*

Truro Gig Club's Royal, built by Ralph Bird, 1988

Rame Gig Club's Spirit of Rame, built by J+G Donne, 1993

St. Ives Gig Club's Porthminster – Looe's gig Ryder
Yealm Gig Club's Hornet

157

Cadgwith's gig Socoa, built by J. Moore, 1990

Newquay's gig Speculation, built by Tom Chudleigh, 1987
(photo: Jack Buzza)

Mounts Bay Gig Club's Sally, built by Peter Foord in 1990

Padstow's Teazer lifting her bow at Nequay

The St. Agnes gig Shah, built by Nicholas Peters of St. Mawes in 1873

St. Mary's gig Serica the first gig to be built this century, built by Tom Chudleigh, 1967

Gibson which has *Cetawayo* in the foreground has been dated by Frank Gibson as circa 1907.

CAPE CORNWALL

There was a gig at Cape Cornwall as early as 1842 when the Cape Cornwall gig is on record as attending the wreck of the schooner *St Austell* on the Brisons (see Wreck & Rescue). The gig bearing the name *Cape Cornwall* was built for the Cape Cornwall gig club in 1990. She was built at Padstow by Peter "Dasher" Reveley and is a "copy" of the Newquay gig *Treffry* at 32' 0" x 4' 10". Colours: white bottom, red boot top, royal blue topsides, orange topstrake.

CORSAIR

Another of the recently built *Treffry* copies. Built in 1991 at Padstow by Peter Reveley and owned by the Port Isaac gig club the 32' 0" x 4'10" Corsair is named after an old Port Isaac gig. Colours: mid blue topside, red bottom, white rubbing strake.

CAMMOE

Probably built by Henry Burt on St. Michaels Mount, *Cammoe* was larger than the other gigs *Mabel* or *Sally* (they were identical gigs built at 24' x 5' 5") *Cammoe* was built with the sole purpose of piloting incoming ships to the Mount.

DARING A St. Agnes gig

The builder and date of build of the St. Agnes gig is unknown. She is remembered for the death of pilot Edwin Jenkins who had rowed out to the Italian barque *Emmanuelle Accame* in January 1895 and later died aboard as a result of exposure (see Wreck & Rescue) *Daring* was left to rot at Periglis.

DART A St. Mary's gig

Another gig owned by Mr. Buxton who ran the pilotage and chandlery business at Porthcressa (see *Cuckoo* also.

DANIEL

An old Scillonian gig. No other information.

DEFIANCE

A St. Ives gig whose name survives having been found on one of the Peters original builders moulds. A gig called *Defiance* did race at Newquay in 1835.

DEFIANCE

A St. Marys gig which may be the same as the above boat. In 1829 her coxswain also put his name to the letter to the Customs regarding the crews of gigs being limited to four. There was also a pilot cutter of the same name registered in St. Marys in 1841. In 1829 her cox was Abraham Stevens.

DOVE of NEWQUAY

Dove was built by William Peters of St. Mawes in 1820. She was built to be faster than *Newquay* but she does tend to be a dirty boat in heavy seas. This has been ascribed to the fact that she is built of broad leaf elm *not* the narrow leaf elm usually used in gig construction.

In 1928 a Newquay crew which was comprised of W. E. Kennedy stroke oar, W. J. Jenkin bow oar, E. Hoare at No. 2, J. Reynolds No. 3, W. Trebilcock No. 4, and R. H. C. Gillis at No. 5 and W. R. Coumbe was cox, when they rowed a double timed measured mile in *Dove* in a time of 6 minutes and 15 seconds. To commemorate this achievement a model of *Dove* built at a scale of 3/4" to the foot was built by Francis Peters of St. Mawes and presented to the County Museum at Truro, where it still is.

Dove is held in Trust at Newquay Rowing Club. She measured 31' 0" x 4' 10" and is coloured white topsides, red bottom, with a red rubbing strake.

DOLLYVARDEN

Was built for the pilots of St. Marys 1873 she was kept in her house at Porthcressa. Much of her working life was spent working with the pilot cutter *Presto*. In 1909 she attended the wreck of the *Plympton* with tragic results. (see Wreck & Rescue)

In her declining days she was used as an impromtu bandstand by the St. Marys Town Band, the conductor, of course, sitting or standing in the cox's seat. When in service the *Dolly Varden* was painted a pale primrose yellow colour. She was reconditioned in 1937 but a later gale floated her out of her gig house and she was irreparably damaged, her planking used to make a punt.

DIDO

A Falmouth "regatta gig" never used for pilotage the *Dido* was of especially lightweight construction. In 1893 in a three gig race at Hayle the *Dido* was second to *Treffry*. The St. Ives gig *Richard*, rowed by a Hayle crew was 3rd.

DOVE of Scilly – A St. Mary's gig.
Peters built but date not known. Not to be confused with the other *Dove* of Newquay. Is on record as assisting the gigs *Blucher* and *Champion* in rescuing the crew of the *Borodino* in 1830 (see Wrecks & Rescue)

DOLPHIN
Built in 1969 by Tom Chudleigh of Scilly for the Islanders of St. Martins. When she was built the *Dolphin* swept the boards at all her races and people found it hard to believe that she was built on the same moulds as *Serica*. However time and changes of crew have shown that whilst *Dolphin* is a good gig, she is only as good as the crew that is rowing her. Tom Chudleigh said that whilst the moulds were the same for both *Dolphin* and *Serica*, when he built *Dolphin* he spaced them differently. The moulds were taken from *Bonnet*. She measures 30' 4" x 4' 9 3/4". Colours: silver grey topsides, with a light blue bottom and a blue rubbing strake. Islanders raised £610 to buld her.

DASHER
Built and named after her buider Peter "Dasher" Reveley in 1989. *Dasher* is owned by the Padstow Gig Club and at 32' 0" x 4' 10" is another copy of the famous *Treffry* of Newquay.

ELAINE A St. Agnes gig.
This gig was unusual inasmuch as it was a 5 oared gig. It was built for Israel Hicks of St. Agnes especially for the relief work of Round Island Lighthouse. Israel Hicks and the gig *Elaine* were the last to contract for keeper relief work with a gig, they also tendered for and got the job of relieving the keepers of the Bishop Rock. It was on one such trip in 1911 that the *Elaine* took part in rescuing the crew of the *Arden Craig* (see Wreck and Rescue). The *Elaine* ended up converted to a motor launch and one night in 1958 she broke free of her mooring in a southerly gale and was irreparably smashed when she drove ashore on the beach near the lifeboat house. Attended the stranded *Roche Castle* in 1911.

EMPEROR
A large gig whose origins are unknown. She was designed principally as a carrier/barge and was kept at Higher Town beach St. Martins. In 1902 with a crew of 14 double banking the oars, she put out to sea with the aim of assisting the *Lofaro* of Naples. However, the weather and sea conditions were so severe she was driven back. (see Wreck

and Rescue). In later years she was fitted with an inboard engine, but sadly this gig ended her days ignominiously providing accommodation for fowls on St. Martins, when she was sawn in two to make a pair of chicken houses!

EVELYN

A Mounts Bay gig built in 1888 by Simmons of Penzance for Croutch of Penzance. Reputedly designed by G. L. Watson. A small gig by Scilly and St. Mawes standards at 19′ 3″ x 5′ 0″ but designed to row six oars in double thole pins. In 1934 the gig was measured up by the late P. J. Oke at that time she was owned in shares by Penzance pilots. The gig was painted black above the waterline with a white rubbing strake, below the waterline she was red.

EXPRESS

An old St. Ives gig mentioned in contemporary reports as being at the wreck of the *Gypsy* on 19th February, 1868 (see Wreck and Rescue).

ENERGY

Was built by students at the Falmouth Technical College Boatbuilding school under the supervision of Ralph Bird. The keel was laid in 1983 and the gig launched in 1985. *Energy* is a copy of the *Treffry* of Newquay at 32′ 0″ x 4′ 10″. In 1986 she was rowed from Falmouth to Plymouth by members of Constantine Sea Angling Club.

ECHO

Name of an old Hayle gig – no other details.

ENDEAVOUR

Another copy of Newquay's *Treffry* built in 1988 by Peter Foord and Tom Dudley *Endeavour* was launched by Richard Sharp, the former Cornwall, Oxford University and England Rugby team fly half and captain. She is owned by Mevagissey Gig Club and is painted cream below the waterline, varnished above. 32′ 0″ x 4′ 10″.

ENERGETIC

Built for Porthleven Gig Club in 1991 by Ralph Bird, this gig is another taken from the lines of Treffry. Colours: yellow topsides, white bottom, black top plank, white rubbing strake 32′ 0″ x 4′ 10″.

This pilot gig is named in memory of the six Richards brothers, Gilbert, Ralph, Billy, John Henry, Perkin and Tom and a visitor friend of theirs, Roy Mewton who put to sea on the 25th June, 1948, from Porthleven in their 25 ton fishing boat P. Z. 114 *Energetic*. Later that night in darkness and poor visibility the *Energetic* was run down and sunk by the 7,218 ton, American Ship, *Chrysanthy Star*, there were only two survivors, Ralph Richards and Roy Mewton and Mr. Mewton died before he reached land. Local rescue services, despite an extensive search, found no trace of the other five Richards brothers.

FORESTER
An old St. Ives gig – no records or other details also the name of a Truro gig.

FLYING FISH
An old Fowey gig mentioned as being a competitor at the 1877 Fowey regatta.

FURY
An old Falmouth gig owned by Leans has given her name to a new gig built 1992.

(NEW) FURY
Built for Falmouth by Ralph Bird of Devoran, in 1992 32' x 4' 10''. Colours: Black topsides, white bottom and rubbing strake, red top-strake. Falmouth's town crest, a double headed eagle is emblazoned in white on the gig's bow.

FEAR NOT
Built by Ralph Bird at Devoran in 1991 this gig is built at 32' 0'' overall but has been pulled in an inch from the Treffry dimensions and has a 4' 9'' beam. She is named after one of the old Devoran gigs. Colours: light blue – topsides, white – bottom, dark blue – top strake, white – rubbing strake.

FORESTER'
Name of an old Truro gig which won the 1st place in the Penzance regatta in 1877.

FLY
Built by Ralph Bird at Devoran and launched 1993 for Newquay Rowing Club. Colours: black – topsides, white – bottom, yellow – rubbing strake. Named after one of the many pilchard seining companies in Newquay that flourished up to 1893 when the last catch of pilchards of any size was made.

FRANKLIN A St. Mary's gig
A Scillonian gig mentioned by Alf Jenkins in "The Scillonian and his boat", no other details given kept at New-Quay St. Mary's.

FORTITUDE
Name of a St. Ives gig, probably a fishing gig however, which capsized near Hayle Bar on 7th November 1900. Her only survivor caught the last train home to St. Ives.

GOOD INTENT
Was built for Newquay in 1975 by Tom Chudleigh on St. Marys. She was built at the same time as the gig *Active* also built for the Newquay Rowing Club, and both were the first "copies" of Newquays *Treffry*.

Good Intent was delayed in her launch because a shortage of suitable timber delayed her building. *Good Intent* was the name of a 19th century Newquay pilchard seining Company. Colours: mid green – topsides, white – bottom, white – rubbing strake.

GYPSY or GIPSY
Was a Scilly built gig, built by Tiddy for St. Agnes pilots in 1858. Gypsy was used on most wreck salvages of her day, so despite her size 28' 0" x 5' 0" she must have been a good boat in most conditions. She is recorded as attending the wreck of the steamer *Castleford* in 1887 (see Wreck and Rescue). Gypsy had the distinction of being the last gig to be used to put a pilot aboard a ship. This was Trinity House pilot Jack Hicks of St. Agnes and the ship was the *Foremost*, on 21st December, 1938. The pilotage free of three pounds, thirteen shillings was paid on Jan 24th 1939.

When *Gypsy* was sold to Padstow Regatta Committee (in 1955) it was discovered that one of her portside planks still had a patch over a hole inflicted by the horns of a bullock from the *Castleford* 68 years previously. On 27th May, 1964 the *Gypsy* was burned at Padstow. R. H. C. Gillis salvaged the copper rudder pintle from the ashes which was later put back into service on the gig *Newquay*.

Originally named *Gipsy* she appears to have had her name "re-spelled" at Padstow. The log book for *Gipsy* is now in the possession of Ralph Bird.

GLEANER'
A Peters built gig made for Tresco's pilots Gillis says that in 1954 *Gleaner* was taken apart by Obediah Hicks and his son Ivor and that the planks were in good enough condition to be reused to make a small boat.

GOLDEN EAGLE a St. Marys gig

Built by Peters in 1870 for the pilots of Bryher. Her name stems from the golden eagle embossed on the back of the gold dollar pieces that paid for her. Earned in salvage money from the American ship *Award* in 1861 (see Wreck & Rescue). The rhyme was penned by the Tresco Abbey boatman Horatio Jenkins:

"The Award from Liverpool did sail
Bound for New Orleans,
She struck upon the rock of Gweal
And went to Smithereens."

Much of the salvaged timber from *Award* went into building Tresco Abbey e.g. the roof of the Dining room and the rooms named Rosevear, Rosevean and Annet. The teak sideboard in the dining room came from her mainmast. *Golden Eagle* is 30' 4" long and was originally 5' 2". In 1953 she was bought by Newquay Rowing Club and had a great deal of renovation work done including a new keel and her beam was altered when she was pulled home to 4' 10". *Golden Eagle* was also renailed at the same time, as she was in 1910 after attending the wreck of the *Minnehaha*. Other wrecks she attended include *Sussex* in 1895, *Brinkburn* in 1898 the *Eric Rickmers* and the *Parame* on the same day in 1899 (see Wreck & Rescue)

GUINIVERE

She is believed to have been a St. Agnes gig, she was lost off the Bishop Rock. After she had put her pilot on board a ship she was taken in tow and was towed under and lost, but her crew were saved.

GALATEA

A pink painted gig and considered to be the fastest gig on St. Martins. An attempt to rescue the crew on the Italian barque *Lofaro* in 1902 included *Galatea* being dragged across the island but to no avail, as weather conditions drove her back (see Wreck & Rescue).

She was worked with the St. Martins registered pilot cutter *Argus* until the *Argus* became too old and unseaworthy and was broken up in 1890. She survived until age and neglect destroyed her and she rotted away in the 1930's.

GIRL I LOVE

Mentioned by R. H. C. Gillis in an article on Newquay gigs she is last mentioned as being at Newquay in a regatta in 1855.

GAZELLE
An old Padstow gig she was varnished but no other details.

GUIDE
Name of an old St. Ives gig which was lost when putting a pilot aboard a ship in St. Ives Bay. She was filled with water and sank when the steamship rolled on to her in the swells. No mention of casualties, presumably the gigs crew were rescued aboard the steamer.

HOUND A St. Mary's gig
Another gig owned by Mr. Buxton pilot gig owner and chandler and kept on Town Beach. On 10th July 1875 *Hound* was ferrying a cricket team home from Tresco when she capsized drowning 4 of the team (see Wreck & Rescue). *Hound* finally rotted away on the grass behind Porthloo beach.

HOPE A St. Mary's gig.
Alf Jenkins is of the opinion that there were two gigs of this name. One a Tresco gig which dates back to at least 1829 when the name *Hope* appears on the letter to the Customs protesting about the rule forbidding any more than 4 to a crew in a gig. This gig also saved the crew of the American Schooner *Susan of Boston* on 29th October 1827, and in 1830 this gig returning from St. Marys with 14 aboard shipped a wave and was sunk. Five of its passengers drowned in the incident. Later, it must have been refloated, because in 1878 a Tresco gig called *Hope* was awarded £25 by the French Government for saving lives from the French ship *Minerve*. The other *Hope* was a St. Marys gig built by Tiddy in the mid 1800's and was generally considered to be the last gig to be rowed to France for the purpose of smuggling. *Hope* was kept when used as a pilot gig, in a house at Porthcressa with the gig *Sultan*.

HORSE
On the 21st May, 1821 the St. Marys gig having put a pilot on a ship the gig was returning to St. Marys with three crew members when she was swamped and sunk by a heavy sea, her crew of three was never seen again. Wreckage of the gig was thrown on St. Mary's beach the following day.

HERO
An old Padstow gig from Cowles yard, painted black but nothing else known.

JOHN HARVEY
Said to have been the name of an old Hayle gig from the 19th Century.

HORNET See UNITY

ISLANDER
Was built by Tom Chudleigh in 1989 and was built to be either rowed in the Islands or against the 32' 0'' gigs from the mainland. When racing from mainland ports, coves and harbours, the *Islander* is shipped to Penzance from St. Mary's on the *Scillonian*. She is 32' x 4' 10'' another clone of the Newquay gig *Treffry*. Colours: maroon topsides, white bottom, white rubbing strake.

There is an excellent documentary video of the building of *Islander* called The *Islander*, filmed by Robin Kewell available from Scillonia Films

ISIS
The gig built for Hayle Gig Club by Ralph Bird in 1993 a copy of *Treffry* the gig is named after a ten oared, self righting lifeboat, the gift of the Oxford University Lifeboat Fund in 1866. *Isis* was built by Forrestt of Limehouse and was transported to Hayle by rail, free of charge. The coxswain of the *Isis* was Edwin Trevaskis who served a total of 23 years in that capacity. *Isis* was on station for 21 years and saved a total of 51 lives. The gig *Isis* is painted a deep cherry red, white bottom, yellow rubbing strake.

JOLLY
A St. Marys gig whose main and only claim to fame is for being stopped from putting to sea by the Customs in 1828 for smuggling offences.

JUNO
A St. Marys gig kept at *Porthcressa* which, with the gigs *Bee* and *Bull*, rescued the crew of the *Victoria* of Exeter 15th February 1838 (see Wreck & Rescue)

On 20th December 1838 *Juno* assisted in rescuing the crew of the brig *Edward Charlton* of Blyth 238 tons, after it had struck on Bartholomew Ledges, and later sank in St. Marys sound. She was assisted by *Unicorn* and the coastguard boat and the pilot cutter *Ranger*.

KLONDYKE
Built in St. Marys for the coastguard service by W. M. Gluyas in 1877.

She was later sold to the St. Agnes pilots who named her, spelling *Klondyke* with a "y". R. H. C. Gillis says she was sold to the Bishop Rock lighthouse attendant on St. Agnes for £8 in 1897. When she was in the Coastguard Service she would not have been named, just numbered. She was presented (1959) originally, by the St. Agnes men to the Valhalla museum, but is now in the St. Marys Museum. She is painted with an all black hull with a pale blue top strake and a white rubbing band. Alf Jenkins gives her dimensions as 29′ 0″ x 5′ 2″ *but* Lyn Tregenna in her "GIG GUIDE" says she measures 27′ 10″ x 5′ 4 ¼″!!? Named after the Gold Rush of 1896 *Klondyke* was used as the doctors boat.

LEO
This was the last gig built in Scilly as a working pilot gig she was built by Samuel Tiddy and his son who later became master of the Hayle built steamer *Lyonesse*. When the father and son team built *Leo*, they built a side each, and Tiddy senior always teased his son that his side was better built than that of his sons. As she would reputedly sail faster on the tack that favoured the side he built than she would on his sons side. *Leo* was kept in a gig house on Rechabite slip. In 1903 she was launched and with the gig *O & M* went to the rescue of the barque *Queen Mab* (see Wreck & Rescue). Her last known owner was someone called W. Rogers.

LION A St. Mary's gig
An old Scillonian gig whose name was included in the 1829 letter to the Customs asking for the law forbidding the crews of gigs to number more than four men. Her coxswain was Charles Phillips – a St. Marys name.

LLOYDS GIGS
These gigs were built for Lloyds of London, the insurance under-writers and marine insurance company. All were built by Peters of St. Mawes and stationed on St. Marys. *Lloyds White* and *Green* were kept on Town Beach and *Lloyds Black* was kept on Porthcressa.

LILY
Built for St. Martins Pilots by Peters of St. Mawes in 1873 she was kept in a house at Old Quay, St. Martins. She was still in St. Martins in good condition, in the mid 1930's but her fate thereafter is not known.

LONG KEEL
A Tresco gig whose house was destroyed to build a slipway for R.A.F. seaplanes in the 1st World War. No details about what happened to the gig.

LITTLE SALLY
A 19th Century Falmouth gig owned by Rusdens.

LIZZIE
A 19th Century Falmouth gig owned by Sawles.

LYONNESSE
Built by Ralph Bird of Devoran in 1988 for the Mounts Bay Gig Club. Named after the legendary "lost land" which mythology says lies between Lands End and the Isles of Scilly. Another copy of the *Treffry* at 32' 0" x 4' 10" painted – golden yellow topside, white bottom, black boot top, white top strake, black rubbing strake.

LION
Name of an old Hayle gig. No other details.

LINNET A St. Martins gig.
A Peters built gig, built at St. Mawes 1830. On the 16th February, 1869 she attended the schooner *Alida* of Veendam (see Wreck and Rescue).

MISTLETOE A St. Mary's gig
This gig was built by Downing Williams and was kept in the same gig house as the *Dolly Varden*. Although the date of her building is unknown, it is known that *Mistletoe* was a five oared gig. Sadly *Mistletoe* was left to rot and was eventually broken up and burnt as firewood. *Mistletoe* was painted green.

MARENE
Built by Peters of St. Mawes in 1871 for the Bryher pilots but nothing is known about this gig other than she was brought to Scilly but that is it.

MARCH
Built by Peters for the Bryher pilots but when, not known. *March* was originally built to beat the *Albion* which was built in 1844 and *Golden Eagle* was built in 1870 to beat March so her build date falls between those years. *March* assisted the gig *Albion* in her epic row to save the survivors of the *Delaware* in 1871 (see Wreck & Rescue). *March* was

not used again for pilotage after the Delaware wrcking and gradually fell apart.

MONARCH A St. Mary's gig
Mentioned on a Regatta programme for the Old Town Cup Race 1913. Attended the wreck of the *Rhodes Castle* in 1912.

MABEL
Built by Burt on St. Michaels Mount in 1867 24′ 0″ 5′ 5″ the gig was painted white with a red strake below the rubbing band.

MEN-A-VAUR
Named after the rock of the same name lying to the north north east of Tresco and West South of Round Island. *Men-a-vaur* was built in 1983 by Gerald Pearn. She is jointly owned by the Tresco and Bryher Rowing Club. *Men-a-Vaur* is a copy of *Shah* at 30′ 2″ 4′ 9″, she is painted with a light blue topside with a white bottom and has a varnished top strake.

MYSTERY
Was built by Peter Foord of Mevagissey in 1991 the origin of her name is in itself a mystery as there have been a number of boats in this area bearing the same name.

Mevagissey had a much loved old rowing lifeboat called *Mystery* in the 1870's. There is a record of a gig called *Mystery* racing at Devonport in 1847 for the Queens plate and £100, it is possible that this was a four oared gig. There was an old four oared gig working out of Charlestown in the 19th Century, the latter two may be the same gig but according to Lyn Tregenna this *Mystery* is named after a 4 oared coastguard gig from Charlestown. She is the same length as *Treffry* copies at 32′ 0″ but an inch narrower at 4′ 9″. Painted with grey – topsides, white – bottom, red – topstrake.

MILLER'S DAUGHTER
Mentioned in S. Baring-Gould's "Cornish Characters and Strange Events" as being a crack Saltash gig owned by one of the Saltash waterside characters, Jacky Gould around 1850 and would have been known by one of Gould's competitors the famous oarswoman Ann Glanville.

MAY GIRL
A four oared Penzance pilot gig which on 6th December 1868 attended the wreck of the barque *North Britain* wrecked in Mounts Bay.

NEWQUAY *(The Old One)*

Built in 1812 by William Peters at St. Mawes. It is incredible to think that when this gig was built George III was on the throne, Napoleon's armies were being forced to retreat from Moscow, and the United States of America declared war on Britain. It was also the year in which Charles Dickens was born!

The *Newquay* is certainly the oldest gig in use today and she is probably the oldest wooden boat in regular use in the world. She has had some renovation work, her keel was renewed in 1955 by Mr. S. Brabyn of Padstow, but she is substantially as she was when she left William Peters yard in 1812. She has never been refastened. She was taken to the Henley Royal Regatta in 1987 and again in 1989.

There is a scale model of *Newquay* built by Frank Peters on display at the National Maritime Museum at Greenwich. Dimensions: 29' 11" 4' 9", painted red – topsides with white rubbing strake and white bottom.

NELLY

An old Falmouth gig owned by Hollacombes.

NIMBLE

A St. Ives gig mentioned attending the wreck of the *Gypsy* at St. Ives in 1868 (see Wreck & Rescue) with the gigs *Express* and *Theodore*.

Nimble and *Theodore* were both raced in local regattas. In 1869 they both raced at the St. Michaels Mount and Marazion regatta. *Nimble* romped home to win the £7 first prize in the race for pilot's or hobbler's gigs with *Theodore* taking second place.

NORMANDY

Often mistaken for a gig this was in fact a ships long boat which may have been salvaged from one of the Islands many wrecks by the Dorrien-Smith family. She was broken-up circa 1950.

NORNOUR

Built for St. Mary's by Gerald Pearn of Looe in 1971 *Nornour* is an "original" gig, her measurements are not taken from any other single gig. She is similar dimension as *Czar* being 1½" narrower in the beam at 5' 0" and 8¾" shorter than *Czar* at 30' 9¼" long. Although she is not as full in the bilge as other gigs she has had a good racing record. In 1972 the *Nornour*, crewed by a mainly under 21 years old crew, was rowed to Roscoff in Brittany in under 37 hours.

O & M

One of St. Agnes' and the Isles of Scilly's greatest gigs, built by the Scillonian shipwright Samuel Tiddy (who also built, amonst others *Leo*). Named *O & M* in honour of its famous owner Obediah Hicks and his wife Mary. This gig was used for many years to relieve and supply the keepers on the Bishop Rock. Amongst the wrecks attended by *O & M* are the *Schiller* which became a total loss with 335 of her passengers and crew out of a total of 372 drowned after striking the Retarrier Ledges on the 7th May, 1875 (see Wreck & Rescue) *O & M* also attended the *Castleford* wrecked on Crebewethan in dense fog on 8th June, 1887 and helped get many of the ships 450 head of cattle on to the Island of Annet. Whilst doing so a bullock leapt from the *Castleford* over the side of the ship and knocked out one side of *O & M's* bow (see Wreck & Rescue).

    O & M was also once dragged across St. Agnes by men and horses to launch from Periglis to rescue the captain of the Italian Ship *Bernardo* from a rock called Old Womans House, the captain Andrea Dapelo was the only one of the crew of 12 to be saved, the rest drowned when their boat capsized. Some accounts give this wreck as occuring in 1880 but it did in fact happen on the 11th March, 1888 (see Wreck & Rescue).

OLD TOWN GIG A St. Mary's gig

Described by Alf Jenkins as "the gig that never had a name". This gig which was kept at Old Town was used to put a pilot aboard a ship in 1821 near to the Gilstone off Penninnis, she shipped a rogue wave which filled and sank her taking six men to their deaths.

PALACE A St. Mary's gig.

Built by Peters of St. Mawes but no dates recorded. She was owned by the Banfield sisters Lizzie and Ada, daughters of the St. Mary's shipping family. *Palace* was kept in the back yard of their house, now called Strand House. The gig was used to go out to the ships at anchor in the roads.

    No records of this gigs demise survive.

PORT QUIN GIG

Name unknown, but reputedly, the Port Quin gig was the fastest gig in her area.

PEACE

An old gig belonging to the Cowles yard, Padstow, it is said to have been varnished but no other information is known.

WILLIAM PETERS

Built by Ralph Bird in 1987 for the Roseland Gig Club, she was appropriately launched by Frank Peters, great grandson of the man she was named after. At 32′ 0″ 4′ 10″ she is a copy of her namesakes masterpiece *Treffry*.

In 1991 The *William Peters* was rowed from St. Mawes to Roscoff, Britanny in 26 hours. Colours: signal red – topsides, white – bottom, white – rubbing strake, name in yellow letters.

PRINCE

Little is known about this St. Mary's gig other than her name and that it was kept on Town Beach.

PORTHMINSTER

A new St. Ives gig built in 1992 and named after one of the towns famous hotels. Colours: bright green – topsides, white – bottom, yellow – rubbing strake, dark blue – top strake.

Built by Peter Foord

PAUL PRY

An old Saltash gig of the Ann Glanville era circa 1850. Her name was found in a book entitled "Cornish Characters and strange events" by S. Baring-Gould in a chapter dedicated to Ann Glanville. *Paul Pry* is described as "a first class craft".

QUEEN

The largest gig in terms of volume, that the Peters of St. Mawes built. Also the last gig to be built at the Peters yard in 1903. She measured 30′ 3″ x 7′ 0″ beam. Built for the pilots of St. Martins, she was used for salvage work and general carrying. Her last remembered use on St. Martins was when she was used to ferry a group of Islanders from Higher Town to Tresco for a concert. When they were part way there someone noticed her old rival the old gig *Empress* leaving Lower Town on a similar mission with a group of people from Lower Town bound for the same concert. Needless to say a race ensued but *Queen's* turn of speed surprised many . . . that is until it was discovered that she had been "assisted" by an outboard motor. She was later sold to Truro where after several bodged attempts to fit engines in her she was abandoned and eventually just fell apart. However the stern post of the Queen was salvaged and is now keenly competed for as a trophy by the Truro Pilot Gig Club. It was presented by Alf Jenkins.

RAILWAY

A Pendreathen gig that was originally owned by Alfred Mumford. Builder not recorded but she may have been built on Scilly. Later she was sold to a Dick Phillips at Old Town but she was never used. After laying around for many years, lack of maintenance, and neglect took its inevitable toll, and she was, eventually, broken up and burnt.

RAILWAY BOAT

This may . . . or may not be the same boat as *Railway*, it could be that one of the railway companies with a ship plying the islands did have a pilot and gig of their own.

RICHARD

An old St. Ives gig, which, in the 1890's, was sold to North Somerset and was taken there on the deck of a ketch.

ROSE

Built for Hayle pilots, but builder unrecorded. It is likely that *Rose* would have been built in Hayle, probably in the shipwrights sheds of Harvey and Co., possibly by apprenticed shipwrights. She was built extremely lightly as a racing gig, as a consequence she was very fast and was banned from competing in many races. However in the 1890 Hayle regatta she is recorded as "easily beating" *Silver Spray* of St. Ives. *Rose* was later sold to Cadgwith where she was smashed to pieces by a boulder dropping on to her from the cliffs. Cadgwith Pilot gig club is to have a new gig called 'Rose' 1994.

RESCUE

An Old Padstow gig painted blue. (mentioned by R. H. C. Gillis)

RIVAL

An old Padstow gig painted green. (mentioned by R. H. C. Gillis)

RASPER

An old St. Ives gig recorded as being capsized and washed ashore whilst attending the wreck of the *Rival* in 1838.

Royal Built for the Truro River Rowing Club by Ralph Bird in 1988. *Royal* is another copy of *Treffry* at 32' 0'' 4' 10''. Painted: royal blue – topsides, white – bottom, yellow – rubbing strake.

RHOS

Built for the Roseland Gig Club in 1989 by Ralph Bird (her name is

Cornish for a headland or promintory). Another gig taken from *Treffry* moulds at 32' 0" 4' 10". *Rhos* was rowed at the Henley Royal Regatta in 1989. Colour: Mid green – topsides, white – bottom.

RIVAL
Built for the "Fowey River Gig Club" in 1989 by Ralph Bird. *Rival* was named after the last ship, (a ketch) to be built in Fowey. Another chip off the old *Treffry* block at 32' 0" 4' 10". Painted: bright red – topsides, white – bottom, black – top strake.

RYDER
Named after Looe's last lifeboat which was on station from 1902, until just after her last call out to the S. S. *Parish* in 1929. This new gig was launched in 1992. Painted: light blue – topsides, white – bottom, varnished – top strake, yellow – rubbing strake. Built by J. & D. Currah

RACHALL or more probably RACHAEL
Given the eccentricity of the spelling in the "Journal of John Pollard of Newlyn 1794–95". The *Rachall* or *Rachael* is recorded as having been "have onshore" and lost on the 28th December 1799 with John Pollard "onbord" (see Wreck & Rescue).

SLIPPEN (or BERNICE)
Built by Peters of St. Mawes in 1830 for the pilots of St. Martins and worked from St. Martins until 1869 when she was sold to the pilots of St. Agnes and her name was changed to *Slippen*. Length 28' 0" x 5' 4". Famous for her rescue of the only survivors of the one and only seven masted schooner *Thomas W. Lawson* in 1907 (See Wreck & Rescue) and also for her part in saving 26 lives from the French Trawler *Cite de Verdun* in 1925 (see Wreck & Rescue). Sold to Newquay Rowing Club in the 1950's she was completely renovated, her survival and renovation being largely due to R. H. C. Gillis, who, with a small group of like minded men, went to Scilly with the sole purpose of preserving the last of the gigs, before they were all either broken up, or left to rot past the point of viability.

In 1975 she returned to Scilly and in 1980 the Newquay Rowing club sold her back to the Islands. She is still in regular use. Colours: orange – topsides, white – top strake, white – bottom.

SHAH A St. Agnes gig
Built by Nicholas Peters of St. Mawes in 1873 the *Shah* was originally built for the pilots of St. Ives. However they considered her build ratio of 30' 2¼" 4' 9" to be too fine. When the Scillonian pilot cutter *Presto*

went to the Peters yard at St. Mawes to collect their new gig *Dolly Varden* they saw the *Shah* and were told that she had been refused by St. Ives pilots. The *Presto's* crew told the pilots on the cutter *Gem* about *Shah* and they went over to see her, after many arguments about the pro's and con's of buying a gig that had been turned down by the St. Ives pilots, they decided to purchase her. She was brought back to Scilly on the deck of the *Gem* and housed at the Cove at St. Agnes.

On the 14th of April 1874 the year after delivering *Shah* the pilot cutter *Gem* broke from her moorings and smashed to pieces on St. Agnes. *Shah* was always considered to be a very fast gig despite the fact that she lost her first race to put a pilot aboard a ship. Piloting till 1929, sold to RHC Gillis 1954 and loaned to Newquay R.C. and in 1955 she was taken to Padstow and had a new keel fitted as well as other renovation work.

In 1963 she was sent back to Scilly on loan and in 1974 *Shah* was included with the gig *Bonnet* in a barter deal with the Newquay Rowing Club in exchange for a new gig. The new gig was called *Active* and was built by Tom Chudleigh on St. Mary's.

Shah's last trip on pilotage duties was July 29th 1929 when pilot Jack Hicks of St. Agnes was put aboard *S.S. Pentreath* bound for Vancouver from Cardiff when she put into Scilly for coal bunkering.

ST. VINCENT A St. Mary's gig

This was a St. Marys gig and worked with the cutter *Atlantic II*, it may well be the case that the gig *St. Vincent* and *Atlantic II* were built by the same builders, William Mumford and W. M. Gluyas. The gig *Klondyke* was built by Gluyas in 1877 and *Atlantic II* was built in 1868. St. Vincent was kept in Custom House Slip. St. Mary's and one of her coxswains was Trinity House pilot Walter Bickford (one of the registered owners of Atlantic II in 1886).

SULTAN A St. Mary's gig.

Was built by Samuel Tiddy and was also owned by the *Atlantic* pilots. She was kept in her house on Porthcressa where the Beach Cafe now stands. She would be used when a ship was seen approaching the Islands from the south She was later sold to the pilots of St. Martin's (1910) who painted her a light blue. She ended her days being washed out of her house on Higher Town Beach during a south easterly gale and was smashed beyond repair.

SUSSEX A Bryher gig.

Built by Nicholas Peters in 1886 the *Sussex* at 30′ 0″ x 5′ 7″ is quite a large but by no means sluggish gig (see Wreck & Rescue 1911 *Roche*

Castle. Built for the pilots of Bryher she was paid for from the money raised by saving life and salvaging from the wrecked steamer of the same name on the 17th December 1885 (see Wreck & Rescue).

Sussex reputedly attended all the wrecks off and near Bryher from the time she arrived and even as late as 1955 this gig was launched into thick fog to search for a ship sounding distress signals near Golden Ball reef. The ship turned out to be the *Mando* and she became a total loss although her crew and their personal possessions were all saved (see Wreck & Rescue). In 1910 the *Sussex* was the first gig to reach the Atlantic Transport Co.'s Liner S. S. *Minnehaha*. The coxswain of the *Sussex*, Richard Thomas Jenkins was invited up to the chartroom to show the Captain of the Minnehaha exactly where she was wrecked. The *Sussex* was always kept on the east side of Bryher and filled a number of roles e.g. she was used to fetch the doctor when required and in 1929 became the wedding barge for Bertha Jenkins when she got married on Tresco. Richard Gillis says she married Reg Vickery of Broadclyst. Alf Jenkins says she married Norman Darling?? In 1968 Ralph Bird fitted *Sussex* with a new keel and the following year in 1969 *Sussex* was rowed from Scilly to Penzance in a record time of 9 hours and 17 minutes Sadly in 1971 *Sussex* was left out on the bank and was blown over and badly damaged and but for Ralph Bird, who bought the wreckage, and painstakingly restored her, she would have been lost.

Sussex is presently on loan to the Porthleven Gig Club and is regularly used. In 1987 she was rowed over the famous mile at Henley.

SERICA

Built by Tom Chudleigh for the men of St. Marys in 1967 and launched by Tom's wife Ethel. *Serica* was built from moulds taken from the old gig *Bonnet* and there was a great deal of debate as to which "side" was the better to replicate. It was found that over the years the wear and tear on *Bonnet* had caused her hull form to distort to the point that the port side bore no resemblance to the starboard side. Eventually one side was chosen and the moulds were made up. The *Serica's* measurements are exactly the same as *Bonnet's* 30' 4'' x 4' 9¾''. On the 21st July, 1968 she was the first gig to be rowed from St. Marys to Penzance for 74 years, her crossing took nine hours and 56 minutes. In 1969 *Serica* was twice taken on attempts to row to France but bad weather meant that both rows had to be called off. In 1972 the St. Marys men's crew used *Serica* to win the Cornish gig championship at Newquay. A feat repeated in 1977, again at Newquay, by the St. Marys ladies crew.

179

STORM
An old Padstow gig built by brothers Richard and John Tredwen. This gig is mentioned in 1858 when it went to the assistance of the S. S. *African* which had broken down off the Doom Bar, Padstow (see Wreck & Rescue)

STEPHEN A St. Agnes gig
This gig was named after her owner pilot Stephen Hicks and is mentioned by Alf Jenkins in his book "The Scillonian and his boat". *Stephen* with the gig *O & M* went to the rescue of the crew of the *Integrity* in 1878 (see Wreck & Rescue)

SWIFT
This gig worked with the pilot cutter of the same name. No details of this gig apart from her name and the whereabouts of her house at Blockhouse, Old Grimsby on Tresco remain.

SILVER SPRAY
An old St. Ives gig well known at regattas all over the county in the late 1800's and early 1900's she was badly damaged in a fire that swept the St. Ives pilot's boathouse in 1917 and had to be destroyed.

SPIRIT OF RAME
Launched in 1993 the *Spirit of Rame* includes some novel build details, her timbers rather than having been notched and jogged to fit the lands in her planking, appear to be fitted as straight timbers, the gap between the timbers and her planking have been filled with wedge shaped fillets. Built for the Rame Gig Club in the time of, (reputedly), only eight weeks, by J. & G. Donne.

SPECULATION
Built for the Newquay Rowing Club in 1987 by Tom Chudleigh of St. Marys. *Speculation* is another copy of Newquay's own *Treffry* at 32' 0" x 4' 10". Colours: white – topside, light blue – bottom.

SOCOA
Built by John Moore of Mevagissey in 1990 for the Cadgwith gig club. *Socoa* was the name of a beautiful French sailing ship that stranded off Cadgwith in 1907. Another *Treffry* clone at 32' 0" x 4' 10".

SALLY
Built by Peter Foord of Mevagissey for the Mounts Bay gig club in 1990. She is the same length as *Treffry* but has been pulled home on

extra inch to give dimensions of 32′ 0″ x 4′ 9″. Colours: white – bottom, orange – topside, black – rubbing strake, white – topstrake.

SOWENNA
The name translates from Cornish to English as "GOOD LUCK" she was built in 1991 by Peter Moore of Mevagissey for the Mevagissey gig club. Colours: Beige – topsides, dark navy blue – bottom, varnished – topstrake. Another of the *Treffry* "buildalikes" at 32′ 0″ x 4′ 10″.

SALLY
Edgar J. Marchand Alf Jenkins maintain the *Sally* is the name of one of the last group of three gigs built by Peters of St. Mawes to row four oars. Date not known, nor eventual owners. The other gigs were called *Mabel* and *Como*. However, I believe this information to be incorrect. A. S. Oliver in his book Boats and Boat building in West Cornwall gives a much fuller account of the gigs *Sally Mabel* and *Cammoe* all of which were built by Henry Burt on St. Michaels Mount. Circa 1867-70. Plans of the *Mabel* are included in this book.

THOMAS
A gig built for the St. Agnes pilots by Peters of St. Mawes in 1838. *Thomas* was the first of the three gigs *Thomas*, *Bee* and *Briton* to arrive at the scene of the wreck of the *Thames* a 500 ton steamship which wrecked on Jackies Rock in 1841 with the loss of 61 of the 65 lives on board. (See Wreck & Rescue). The figurehead of the *Thames* is in the Valhalla museum.

TEAZER (ST. IVES)
Name given to an old St. Ives gig – no other records survive.

TEAZER (PADSTOW)
Name of an old Padstow gig which in its livery of black represented Cowles yard.

TEAZER (NEWQUAY)
The gig formerly known as *Zoe Treffry* was unofficially at first dubbed *Teazer* but the name stuck, I suppose to distinguish it from Newquays other gig the *Treffry*. *Teazer* (or *Zoe Treffry*) survived until 1915 when it was "recycled" to become the roof of a chicken house in Newquay.

TEAZER (PADSTOW (1988)
Built by Peter Foord and Tom Dudley in 1988 this "new" *Teazer* was named after the old Padstow gig from Cowles yard and of course the

Teazer is almost as important as the "Obby Oss" in Padstows annual May Day celebrations, it is the Teazer that inspires, encourages, cajoles and partners the Obby Oss in its dance every year.

The gig *Teazer* proudly displaying the cross of St. Piran on its bow is another copy of the *Treffry* at 32' 0" x 4' 10" and is painted with white topsides, black bottom, and a black topstrake.

TOPSY

The name of one of Scilly's coastguard gigs and also the coastguard cutter. She was kept in her house beneath the coastguard house in Thoroughfare, St. Mary's

TOM SAYERS

An old Port Isaac gig which ignominiously ended her life as a grain and fodder bin in a barn on a farm near Port Isaac.

THEODORE

An old St. Ives gig which, in 1868 attended the wreck of the *Gypsy* in St. Ives Bay along with the gigs *Express* and *Nimble* (see Wreck & Rescue). At the 1869 regatta in Mounts Bay *Theodore* is reported as having come 2nd to the gig *Nimble* in the race for pilots or hobbler gigs.

TREFFRY

Built by William Peters of St. Mawes in 1838 for the *Treffry* Company of Newquay. Treffry was built to be Newquays fastest gig and has frequently lived up to that expectation. She is a fine lined gig that comes into her own when being pushed to her limits, a good boat in any conditions, it is said that the harder she is driven the more she will lift.

Treffry has become the "mother" of many of the new gigs built in the past couple of decades, her lines being generally accepted as perfection. In the 1950's *Treffry* received a new keel and in 1989 John Moore of Mevagissey replaced all her timbers, this had been done before, only on this occasion John Moore "joggled" the frames to fit the lands on the planks as would have been originally done. The thwarts and knees were also replaced. *Treffry* looks set fair for at least another 151 years of use after this work!

In 1991 the *Treffry* was taken to the traditional boat rally festival at Henley. (More of *Treffry* in the chapter on the Peters of St. Mawes). In 1977 Paul Shweiss of the Clinker Boat Works, Tacoma, Washington, U.S.A. built a reproduction of *Treffy* for the Eureka Rowing Club of California.

UNICORN
Recorded with the pilot cutter *Ranger* and the gig *Juno* and also the coastguards boat as going to the assistance of the brig *Edward Charlton* which was wrecked on the Bartholomew Ledges on 20th December 1836 (see Wreck & Rescue).

UNITY
Built for Newquay Rowing Club by the St. Marys boatbuilder Tom Chudleigh in 1978. Another copy of Newquays own *Treffry* at 32' 0'' x 4' 10'' *Unity* was named after one of the old Newquay Pilchard Seining Companies of the last century. On 7th May, 1987 the *Unity* was rowed from Newquay to Scilly, a distance of 57 miles in 11 hours and 20 minutes. She left Newquay at 3.00 a.m. and arrived in St. Mary's at 2.20 p.m. George Northey a stalwart gig enthusiast and one of the men responsible for saving and restoring the Scillonian gigs in the 1950's and rekindling the resurgence of interest in gig racing in recent years, and the chairman of the Newquay Rowing Club, was given the honour of coxing *Unity* over the homeward stretch.

As *Unity* she was painted with a white bottom and black topsides. However in 1992 *Unity* was sold to a new home on the river Yealm in Devon. She has now been renamed *Hornet* and repainted with yellow topsides, white bottom, with a black rubbing strake and the name *Hornet* in a white bow flag.

VENUS
The name of a Bryher gig which in 1828 was forbidden by the Customs and Excise from putting to sea because of smuggling offences.

VIOLA
The name of the gig used by Ann Glanville and her ladies crew when they raced against teams of "sailors, amateurs and occasional rowers" at Hull, Yorkshire in 1847.

VIXEN
An old Padstow gig which represented Rowles yard, the *Vixen* was varnished.

VICTOR
An old Padstow gig but no other details.

VENTURE
Name of an old Hayle gig but no other details.

WASP
The name of an old St. Agnes, Isles of Scilly gig, no other details.

WHALER
The name of a St. Marys gig kept at Pendreathen, no other details.

WARSPITE
The name of an old Padstow gig built at Devonport by apprenticed shipwrights in the Royal Naval Dockyards.

WINGFIELD
The last of a dynasty *Wingfield* was the name of the last six oared pilot gigs to be built by the Peters family at St. Mawes.

WILLIAM
An old St. Ives gig Circa 1842 mentioned as having gone to the assistance of the barque *Bosphorus* bound with a general cargo to Jamaica the *William's* pilots managed to bring her safely into anchor and a pilotage claim for £400 was eventually settled for £150.

ZELDA A Tresco gig
Was paid for with money raised from salvage and rescue work on the ship of the same name wrecked on Maiden Bower in 1874 (see Wreck & Rescue). Built in 1874 by Nicholas Peters of St. Mawes for the pilots of Tresco, the *Zelda* went out to recover the body of the mate of the four masted barque *Falkland* which tore her bottom out on the Bishop Rock in 1901 (see Wreck and Rescue) The crew on this mission were, Horatio Jenkins (cox) Wm. Woodcock (stroke) John Woodcock, Wm. Hartley, James Woodcock, Obediah Hicks and Coast Guard Kent.

In 1955 *Zelda* was purchased by the Padstow Regatta Com- mittee but was later damaged beyond repair when a lorry backed into her on the quay. Sections of her bow and stern were salvaged and now adorn a restaurant in St. Marys.

ZOE TREFFRY
Was the name of a famous Newquay gig which was later to be renamed *Teazer* It was reputedly sold in 1915 for a sovereign and ended her life as the roof of a fowls house.

ZEUS
Built for Par Pilot Gig Club by J+D Currah, launched by Brian Trenoweth, April 1994. Another copy of Treffy at 32' x 4'10''. Colours – Orange top strake, white rubbing strake. Burgundy topsides, white bottom.

EVOLUTION, NEAR EXTINCTION, RESURRECTION & PROGRESSION

The start line, St. Mary's, Isles of Scilly, 1993 Championship

The bow oar being "tossed" when rounding a racing point to enable a sharper turn

Pilot gigs have always been well travelled craft. Many gigs were used for smuggling in the last century. John Nance, a St Martin pilot, is reputed to have made 25 trips to Roscoff in Brittany in an open gig on smuggling trips. The St Marys gig *Jolly* was stopped from putting to sea in 1828 for smuggling offences as was the Bryher gig *Venus*. The gig *Bull* from St Marys met a tragic end in Smith Sound after setting out on a "free trading" trip. The only remains of the *Bull* was a piece of wood that was washed ashore it was recognised as being from the *Bull* as it had only recently been fitted.

Gigs were also rowed considerable distances to secure pilotages St. Ives and Hayle gigs often ventured as far as Lundy in order to intercept Colliers bound from South Wales. The gigs of St Mawes and Falmouth could be found as far up channel as the Eddystone light and beyond and as far and, probably further to the west as the Lizard.

No trick was missed to steal a march on the opposition. The St Mawes pilots for example often kept their gigs in a secluded cove near St Anthony light on the entrance of the Carrick roads.

From this vantage point they could keep an eye on the activities of the Falmouth gigs and have a head start in them. The cove was known in past years as Gig Hole, but it is now known as Long Boat Hole.

Many old regatta programmes give the names of gigs and show that gigs were often transported considerable distances in order to compete for the considerable amounts of prize money on offer. In 1877 the *Shah* was brought over from Scilly by a St Ives crew to race at Hayle regatta.

In the 1877 regatta at Fowey, the Newquay gigs *Treffry* and *Dove* took 2nd and 3rd places respectively.

Also in 1877 at the Penzance regatta the Truro gig *Forester* beat the

Gigs at Hayle Regatta 1904

St Agnes gig *Shah* and the St Ives gig *Richard*. The Newquay gig *Treffry* was rowed to Hayle for the 1893 regatta the crew set off from Newquay on the Friday evening, won the regatta on Saturday and on Sunday morning rowed back to Newquay arriving in time for a late lunch. In modern times transporting a gig on a purpose road trailer is a comparatively easy task; but years ago it meant several days travel on a horse drawn cart. Many of the Peters built gigs were transported in this way to all parts of the country, or were placed on the deck of a sailing vessel as in the case of the *Shah* which was taken to St Agnes on the deck of the pilot cutter *Gem*. *Czar* was taken to Bryher, by sea all the way, she was towed by the squire of St Mawes yacht *Sea Snake*. *Sussex* was rowed to Falmouth and from there to Penzance she was transported by cart; from Penzance to the Isles of Scilly she was transported on the deck of a ship.

In recent years gigs have been taken over to Brittany by shipment from Plymouth to Roscoff via Brittany Ferries on many occasions to complete at various festivals etc. Scillonian gigs frequently complete with the Breton pilot boats both at home and in Brittany and several modern gigs have made the cross channel trip to France under sail or oars or both. The *William Peters* was rowed from St Mawes to Roscoff in 26 hours in 1991.

Nornour from St Marys undertook the trip from the Scillies to Roscoff in 37 hours in 1972.

The *Serica* was rowed from St Marys to Penzance on 21st July 1968 the first attempt in 74 years. The following year two attempts were made to sail and row *Serica* to France, but adverse weather conditions resulted in both attempts being abandoned. The first attempt which started on 10th May 1969 was abandoned because of rough sea conditions which resulted in the *Serica* shipping too much water. The second attempt with the *Serica* partly decked in forward, got about half way before slow progress and sea sickness took its toll.

In 1969 a crew made up from members of Constantine Sea Anglers Club rowed the *Energy* from Falmouth to Plymouth on a sponsored row.

Several gigs have been invited to row at the Henley Royal Regatta. In 1987 the gigs *Sussex* and *Newquay* were rowed over the Henley regatta course. In 1989 *Rhos* and *Buller* were invited to Henley as was the *Treffry* in 1991. Gigs have always raced, their shape has evolved over hundreds of years probably with each succeeding gig being a refinement on its peredecessors. This evolution, it is generally accepted reached its zenith with the Newquay gig *Treffry* and it is from the *Treffry* that the plans and moulds for most of the 20th Century gigs have been taken. However this refinement is still taking place as with

191

the gigs built by Ralph Bird, all of which are "copies" of *Treffry* but none are identical, the beam on some of these vessels is 4' 9" on others it is 4' 10" the bow shape is sharper on some and less so on others etc.

Gigs races, traditionally, were rowed over an anti clockwise triangular course of about six miles, but nowadays the courses tend to be shorter and because of the number of gigs competing, (often 20 or more) the course is likely to be a straight line dash.

The stroke rate is usually between 35 and 42 strokes per minute. In the 1990 Newquay Championships the Scillies Mens "A" crew rowed twice around the 2 mile course at an astonishing 40 strokes to the minute to win the championship.

Each cove and port with a gig usually holds a regatta during the season, which starts in May and ends in September. The major meetings are the Championships in the Scillies and at Newquay. But each meeting is special and each regatta has its attractions or detractions depending on whether you are rowing or spectating. There are special races too. Amongst which are the Morley Trophy raced for in the Isles of Scilly as is the ladies Gallaher Cup. Whilst on the mainland, Newquay Rowing Club holds a gig race every year using only the old gigs *Dove Treffry* and *Newquay*. It is considered a great honour to be chosen for one of the 3 crews to race in the "Silver gig" race. The trophy, which is rarely seen, apart from the day of the race, is a solid silver scale model of a pilot gig presented by the late T. A. Reed in 1992. During the rest of the year the trophy is usually kept in the banks vaults. The average winning time is about 40 minutes.

Every year since 1979 there has been a gig race from St Mawes to Restronguet, named after the man who started it, this is the Ralph Bird gig race.

There is now hardly a cove or port in Cornwall that has not got a gig, the sport has an enormous following when one considers that each gig has a crew of six rowers and a typical regatta will have races in 6 or so categories and there will probably be over 20 gigs competing, in crews alone there are frequently over 500 people people converging on a coastal town somewhere in Cornwall most weekends of the summer and probably as many or more spectators, followers and supporters. I doubt if the three men, Richard Gillis, Tom Pryor and George Northey who made the trips to the Scillies in the 1950's to inspect and purchase the remaining Scilly gigs *Slippen*, *Bonnet*, *Golden Eagle* and *Shah* realised then how the sport would flourish. It was to be a fortuitous visit, had Messrs Gillis, Northey and Pryor not purchased these gigs and brought them to the mainland for restoration they would have, in all probability gone the same way as many of

Gig race off St. Mary's – Gibson photo – gigs from foreground, Cetawayo, St. Agnes; Leo, St. Mary's; Bonnet, Tresco; Lloyds, St. Mary's; Dolly Varden, St. Mary's; Lily, St. Martin's. This photo may be of Cetawayo's last and final trip to sea, she fell apart after her last race in 1902

the other fine gigs on the Islands and been either broken up for firewood or been left to rot.

In 1956 Newquay had 7 gigs and only *Czar*, *Sussex*, *Campernell*, *Klondyke* remained in the Scillies *Gipsy* and *Zelda* having been bought by Padstow. Both the last two boats have now gone *Zelda* was smashed beyond repair when a lorry reversed into her and *Gipsy*, or *Gypsy* as she was renamed at Padstow was left to rot and was finally burned at Padstow on 27th May 1964.

From this date the decline was halted and new gigs began to be built until now there are 40 or more gigs either in existence or under construction. Following Richard Gillis and his Newquay colleagues efforts to save the gigs, and the work done, particularly by Gillis, to establish the Newquay gigs for the 1951 Festival of Britain celebrations, Ralph Bird, who has rowed for Newquay and in the Scillies took up the baton. In the 1980's he was instrumental in bringing gig racing to the South Coast of Cornwall. To date he has built 13 new gigs, advised on, and supervised the construction of others, and no doubt will long continue to improve on this tally. Gigs and gig racing once destined to be a thing of the past has risen from the ashes of obscurity and looks set to be with us for many years to come. A particularly Cornish sport with its feet in history and head looking toward the future.

A six-oared gig race at St. Mawes in the year of Queen Victoria's Jubilee

Taken from "The Graphic" 1887

Most of the picturesque fishing villages along the Cornish coast hold an annual regatta where the best sailing boats and rowing crews meet again and again. Perhaps no harbour along the coast is more favourably situated for such purposes than St. Mawes, and it numbers among its inhabitants as able and daring pilots, and hardy fishermen as are anywhere to be met. The boys find their way into and onto the sea almost as soon as they can walk.

This season a gentleman suggested that two crews might be found to row the sea-going six-oared pilot gigs of the port, one to be composed of Old Boys and the other to be Young Boys whose united ages were to show a remarkable disparity. The figure suggested was 500 years, and the two crews were selected and matched who turned out to be strong and able boatmen, and by no means unworthy competitors. The united ages of the young crew totalled 79 while the veterans reached the wonderful aggregate of 580, two of 90 years each.

Some hours before the time of the race a steamer, having on board the Mayor and Corporation, and a large number of gentlemen from the city of Truro, who had been beating the water bounds, steamed up the harbour and expressed a desire to see the special race. As they could not wait until the time appointed for the race the crews consented to oblige with a preliminary contest and a good round was marked off. At the firing of a gun the youngsters dashed off and by a little clever steering and frequent spurts managed to round the first mark about a length ahead, but on coming up the straight the Old Boys steadied down to a long powerful stroke, soon collared them, then drew ahead and were never caught again. The visitors were astonished at the rowing powers displayed by the veterans, and the bow oarsman 90 years old came on board, thankfully received an extra prize. This old salt explained that he had never rowed or sailed in a regatta before, but that he was resolved to turn his attention in that direction, and accepted an invitation to join in a contest at a subsequent date.

Our engraving is drawn from a photograph by Mr. Frederick Argall, High Cross, Truro, and forwarded by Mr. Hugh Price by whom the above information was supplied and represents the crews in the subsequent and more severe race at the moment the gun was fired announcing the veterans to be the winners a second time by a good lead. This was a gamely rowed contest, and Mr. J. C. Kennerley, J.P., who had witnessed it from his yacht invited the Old Boys and Young Boys to come on board and take tea, an invitation to which they cheerfully responded, when the old men by their lively wit and and robust health made it difficult to believe they were on the shady side of life before the Jubilee period we had celebrated commenced. When told their exploits would appear in the Graphic they said it would be something to talk about when they were old.

An account of a remarkable gig race which took place in 1887 at St. Mawes between a gig crewed by a young crew whose ages totalled 79 years and a gig crewed by . . . older men whose ages totalled 580 years. This account was reprinted in "A Sea Miscellany of Cornwall and the Isles of Scilly" by Richard Gillis. There is a photo of the crew in the St. Mawes Yacht Club

WHAT, WHERE, WHEN, SOME OF THE GIGS AND SOME OF THE BUILDERS WHO BUILT THEM

Bonnett, built by William Peters, 1830

Some of the Pilot gig builders and *some* of the gigs attributed to them with the year of launching if known

THE PETERS FAMILY OF POLVARTH NR. ST. MAWES

Newquay	1812	Albion	1844	Czar	1879
Dove	1820	March	1850	Sussex	1886
Bonnet	1830	Linnet	1869	Gleaner	date unknown
Slippen	1830	Golden Eagle	1870	Circe	date unknown
Dove (of Scilly)	1830	Marene	1871	Palace	date unknown
Defiance	1835	Dolly Varden	1873	Queen	date unknown
Bull	1838	Lily	1873	Wingfield	date unknown
Bee	1838	Shah	1873	Lloyds White	date unknown
Treffry	1838	Zelda	1874	Lloyds Green	date unknown
Thomas	1838	Cetewayo	1870's	Lloyds Black	date unknown.

RALPH BIRD OF DEVORAN

Buller	1986	Rhos	1989	Fear Not	1991
William Peters	1987	Rival	1989	Fly	1993
Royal	1988	Ann Glanville	1990	Isis	1993
Lyonnesse	1988	Energetic	1991	Fury	1992

New gig for Cadgwith commenced construction Spring 1994, to be named Rose.

Gigs racing in the 1993 Gig Championships, May 1993, Isles of Scilly
(photo: Jack Buzza)

TOM CHUDLEIGH OF ST. MARYS ISLES OF SCILLY

Serica	1967	Good Intent	1975	Islander	1989
Dolphin	1969	Unity now			
		Hornet	1978		
Active	1974	Speculation	1987		

SAMUEL TIDDY, ISLES OF SCILLY

Gipsy	1959	Leo	O & M
Hope	1850's	Sultan	

HENRY BURT, ST. MICHAEL MOUNT

Cammoe	Mabel	Sally

PETER "DASHER" REVELEY

Cape Cornwall	Dasher	1989	Corsair	1991

TREDWEN BROTHERS, PADSTOW

Arrow	Circa 1850
Storm	Circa 1850

W. M. GLUYAS, ISLES OF SCILLY

| St. Vincent | 1870 | Klondyke | 1877 |

PETER FOORD AND TOM DUDLEY

| Endeavour | 1988 | Teazer | 1988 |

PETER FOORD

| Mystery | 1991 | Sally | 1990 | Porthminster | 1992 |

GERALD PEARN

| Men-a-Vaur | 1983 | Nor Nour | 1971 |

SIMMONS PENZANCE

Evelyn

FALMOUTH TECHNICAL COLLEGE BOAT BUILDING COURSE

Energy 1983

JOHN MOORE

Socoa   1990

J. & D. CURRAH

| Ryder | 1992 | Zeus | 1994 |

New gig for Yealm Pilot Gig Club to be launched August 1994.

R. N. DOCKYARD, DEVONPORT

Warspite Circa   1860

J. & G. DONNE

Spirit of Rame   1993

PETER MOORE

Sowenna 1991

PAUL SCHWEISS OF THE THE CLINKER BOAT WORKS, TACOMA, WASHINGTON, U.S.A.

Copy of Treffy 1977.

THOMAS OF ST. IVES

Specialized in building fishing gigs, but probably also built pilot gigs.

DOWNING WILLIAMS

Built the St. Mary's gig, 'Mistletoe'.

BOATBUILDING YARDS THAT HAD THEIR OWN GIGS

BRAGDONS (FALMOUTH)
Black Diamond

FOX'S (FALMOUTH YARD)
Black Ball

LEANS (FALMOUTH YARD)
Fury

COWLES (PADSTOW YARD)
Hero
Peace
Teazer

SAWLES (FALMOUTH YARD)
Lizzie

RUSEDENS (FALMOUTH YARD)
Little Sally

HOLLACOMBES (FALMOUTH YARD)
Nelly

ROWLES (PADSTOW YARD)
Vixen

List of Club Secretaries
names and addresses

Cadgwith
Steve Collins, Ocklynge, St. Ruan, Ruan Minor, Helston. (0326) 290764.

Cape Cornwall
Peter Angwin, Star Inn, St. Just. (0736) 788767.

Caradon
Martin Langdon, Maydowne, Longcoombe Lane, Polperro, Looe PL13 2PL. (0503) 72269

Charlestown
Susan A. Orchard
111 Phemyssick Road, St. Austell PL2 3TZ. (0726) 69408

Devoran
Mrs. Jo Chirgwin, 27 Tremain Close, Devoran. (0872) 865707.

Falmouth
Simon Culliford, 20 Boscundle Avenue, Goldenbank, Falmouth. (0326) 313435.

Fowey
Maurice Hunkin, 7 Cobbs Well, Fowey. (0726) 832001

Hayle
Chris Barrett, 10 Ellis Close, Hayle. (0736) 756516

Isles of Scilly
Diane Mumford, Veronica Lodge, St. Mary's, Isles of Scilly. (0720) 22585.

Looe
John Currah, 5 Restormel Road, East Looe PL13 1EJ. (0503) 264007.

Mevagissey
Sue Croft, Fernlea Cottage, Rosemellyn, Roche, St. Austell PL26 8LB. (0726) 890743.

Mounts Bay
Mrs. S. Richards, "Compton,", Cockwells Lane, Cockwells, Penzance TR20 8DB. (0736) 740426.

Newquay
Ian Armstrong, 30 Bonython Road, Newquay. (0637) 872418.

Padstow
Lindsey Olds, 6 Highlanes, St. Issey, Wadebridge. (0841) 540455.

Porthleven
Ted Gundry, 10 Peverell Road, Porthleven TR13 9DL. (0326) 561784.

Port Issac
Mark Provis, Leat House, Church Hill, Port Isaac. (0208) 880258.

Rame
John Farley, "Penlee" Lodge, Cawsand, Torpoint. (0752) 823486.

Roseland
Mr. R. Howard, "Banks", Trelawney Road, St. Mawes. (0326) 270797.

St. Ives
Phil Hughes, Nineven Cottage, Fore Street, Lelant, St. Ives. (0736) 752012.

Truro
Eileen Denton, "Solarium," Pill Creek, Feock, Truro. (0872) 864687.

Yealm
Phil Carter, Futtocks End, The Green, Newton Ferrers, Devon. (0752) 872189.

Bibliography

More building Clasic Small Craft John Gardiner
Inshore Craft of Britain in the days of Sail and Oar Edgar March
Boatbuilding Howard Chapelle
Cornish Shipwrecks (The South Coast Vol. 1) Clive Carter
Cornish Shipwrecks (The North Coast) Clive Carter
Gigs and Cutters of the Isles of Scilly A. J. Jenkins
Wreck & Rescue round the Cornish Coast Cyril Noall & Graham Farr
Wrecks around our coast W. F. Ivey
Devon & Cornwall Notes & Queries Journal Autumn 1988
Devon & Cornwall Notes & Queries Journal Spring 1988
Gig Racing in the Isles of Scilly Frank Gibson
Boats & Boat building in West Cornwall A. S. Oliver
Glossary of Cornish Sea Words R. Morton-Nance
HEVVA! Cornish Fishing in the days of sail Keith Harris
Cornwall & Isles of Scilly Gig Guide Lyn Tregenna
A Sea Miscellany of Cornwall and the Isles of Scilly Richard Gillis
The Story of St. Ives Cyril Noall
A History of Gerrans & Portscatho 1700–1830 Hilary Thompson
The Pilot Gigs of Cornwall and the Isles of Scilly R. H. C. Gillis
The pilot gigs of Newquay R. H. C. Gillis
The History of the Cornish Copper Company W. H. Pascoe
The Scillonian Magazine Various articles/various editions
Shipwrecks of the Isles of Scilly Charlotte Dorien Smith
Wrecks of the Isles of Scilly Juliet du Boulay
Sail and Oar John Leather
The Scillonian and his boat Alf Jenkin
May day Sheila Bird
Cornish lights and shipwrecks Cyril Noall
Falmouth to Helford Frank Pearce

Cornish Seines and Seiners Cyril Noall
The Fortunate Islands R. L. Bowley
A Cornish Anthology A. L. Rowse
The Cornish Magazine Articles Aug. 1960
The Cornish Magazine Feb. 1960
The Cornish Magazine Mar. 1960
The Cornish Magazine May 1962
The Cornish Magazine Feb. 1963
The Cornish Magazine Jan 1964
The Love of Ships Tre Tryckare
Shipwrecks around the Scillies Gibsons
The Savage Sea Photographs Gibsons
Haydn's Dictionary of Dates and Universal Information Vincent
Cornwall's early lifeboats Cyril Noall
The Story of St. Ives Cyril Noall
Cornish Characters and Strange Events S. Baring-Gould (1908)
Shipwrecks on the Isles of Scilly F. E. Gibson 1971
Shipwrecks around the Isles of Scilly Isles of Scilly Museum Publication No. 3
Royal Institute of Cornwall Journal 1992 Articles by P. A. S. Pool
Sailing Drifters Edgar J. March
The Cornish Coasts and Moors A. G. Folliott
Old Newquay S. Teague Husband
Cornish Seafarers A. K. Hamilton Jenkin
The Ports & Harbours of Cornwall Richard Pearse
Around the Waterways of the Fal Sheila Bird
The Mevagissey Companion Sheila Bird
Cornish Life Magazine July 1987 Article by Sue Morris
Cornish studies for Schools Article by S. Callan